WADSWORTH PHILOSOPHERS SERIES

ON

ARISTOTLE

Garrett Thomson
College of Wooster

Marshall Missner
University of Wisconsin, Oshkosh

WADSWORTH
CENGAGE Learning

Australia • Brazil • Japan • Korea • Mexico • Singapore • Spain • United Kingdom • United States

On Aristotle
Garrett Thomson,
Marshall Missner

For product information and technology assistance, contact us at **Cengage Learning Customer & Sales Support, 1-800-354-9706**

For permission to use material from this text or product, submit all requests online at **www.cengage.com/permissions**
Further permissions questions can be emailed to **permissionrequest@cengage.com**

ISBN-13: 978-0-534-57607-3

ISBN-10: 0-534-57607-9

Wadsworth
20 Davis Drive
Belmont, CA 94002
USA

Cengage Learning is a leading provider of customized learning solutions with office locations around the globe, including Singapore, the United Kingdom, Australia, Mexico, Brazil, and Japan. Locate your local office at **www.cengage.com/global**

Cengage Learning products are represented in Canada by Nelson Education, Ltd.

To learn more about Wadsworth, visit **www.cengage.com/wadsworth**

Purchase any of our products at your local college store or at our preferred online store **www.cengagebrain.com**

Printed in the United States of America
5 6 7 14 13 12 11 10

Contents

1

Aristotle's World

To us, it would be a strange and alien world. A place where people appease powerful gods by killing animals; where fortune-tellers burn oxtails to determine what the future will be; where slavery is taken for granted; and where women are generally confined to their homes and are infrequently seen in public. It was a place where few people can read, and crowds gather to hear poets recite the long epics of Homer from memory.

This was the Greek world of Aristotle. Of specific interest to us is the intellectual culture of ancient Greece. While we take the influence of two thousand years of Christianity for granted, the Greeks had no such background. They were polytheists who believed in a vast hierarchy of gods, spirits, demigods, and nymphs. They had no sacred text that provided them with commandments to obey, accompanied by descriptions of rewards or punishments in an after-life.

Another important difference between intellectual life in ancient Greece and our own is that knowledge was not yet compartmentalized into different areas, such as the natural sciences, social sciences and humanities. We assume a fragmentation of knowledge into disciplines, each with its own special methods, but no such notion was established in Greece, and it was Aristotle, more than anyone, who first suggested and then worked out the different methods that are needed to study different questions.

More than anything, we take for granted a vast and complex background of accumulated knowledge that the Greeks did not have.

1

Aristotle's World

For example, we know that the moon is roughly 250,000 miles from the Earth; we assume that animals and plants are classified into species; and we have learned that the water of the rivers comes from the sea. All of these things were discovered and worked out after Aristotle's time. If we want to know the distance between the Earth and the Sun, we can look it up in a book. For Aristotle there was no such book, and anyone interested in this question would have to find the answer without the use of any special instruments.

Without this background knowledge, and without the constraint of fragmented disciplines, there was a whole world to understand and explore. Generally, the intellectual culture of ancient Greece was very optimistic and bold. It lacked the cynicism and self-doubt that sometimes plagues our age. This positive attitude became a characteristic of the Greeks that Aristotle inherited. The Greeks had an extraordinary confidence that they could understand the world in all of its aspects through the application of their own intellectual capacities.

While Aristotle's world was very different than ours in many respects, we should not conclude that his work is only of historical interest. There are at least three very good reasons to study his work. First, despite the differences, many of his problems still concern us. However, he did not make our contemporary assumptions when he approached these problems. Studying Aristotle gives us the opportunity to see contemporary problems without contemporary assumptions. For example, when we consider the relation between the mind and the body, our views are permeated by 2,000 years of Christian teaching about the soul. We also incorporate into our view, the idea that matter is inert, a theory which first developed in the late sixteenth century. Aristotle did not make these assumptions, and so his discussion of the mind-body problem is not only interesting, but useful; it may provide us with clues to help resolve the issue.

Aristotle's different background is especially important to us in ethics and politics. In these areas the ancients may have had more wisdom than we do, and we should try to appreciate these "new" ideas and approaches which come from our past. Aristotle was especially insightful in answering the question of how we can live a good human life, both individually and together in a community. Some contemporaries think that Aristotle provided the best answers on these questions that have ever been developed.

A second reason for studying Aristotle is that, as different as his world was from ours, his work has played an enormous role in shaping our outlooks and ideas. It was Aristotle's division of knowledge into

2

different subject matters that we still generally accept. It was Aristotle who through the work of Thomas Aquinas had an important influence on the development of Christian theology and ethics. It was Aristotle who emphasized the role of systematic empirical investigation that is one of the basic foundations of our science. In many areas of knowledge we still rely on concepts that Aristotle first developed.

So, while Aristotle's world seems alien and strange. it is not completely removed from us. In many ways. his world is our parent. and like all parents, while they may seem somewhat bizarre, there are still things we can learn from them.

There is a third reason for studying Aristotle – the nature of the man himself. He had a rare combination of qualities – of being very pragmatic. and at the same time. sensitive to theoretical issues. He recognized the importance of both empirical evidence and fundamental principles. So, his thought is often both subtle and commonsensical. Furthermore. he must have had a furiously energetic and fertile mind. His literary output was immense. and extraordinarily varied. He studied nearly all areas of knowledge and invented new ones.

2
A Life that Changed the World

In 347 B.C Plato died. Aristotle was about 37 years old. His whole adult life had been spent in Plato's academy, studying under the powerful influence of the great teacher. Born in 384 B.C, Aristotle had been sent to the Academy at the age of 17. He became one of Plato's three main pupils. As such, Aristotle probably taught and lectured. He wrote several dialogues which are now lost, except for some fragments. During this first period of his adult life, he may have also started work on the *Categories* and may have already begun his empirical studies in biology.

When Plato died, his nephew, Speusippus, became head of the Academy. This appointment was probably very much to Aristotle's disliking, for he too was candidate for the post. Furthermore, the new head would continue the emphasis on the mathematical model of knowledge and Aristotle was probably uneasy with that focus, having already initiated his more empirical studies of nature.

He left Athens and embarked on a new independent life of intellectual and scientific exploration. This marks the second and middle period of his adult life, during which Aristotle's own way of doing philosophy started to gain clarity and strength.

Invited by a former student of the Academy, Hermias, Aristotle moved to Assos, in the district of Mysia, in what is today northwestern

Turkey. Remarkably, Hermias was once a slave and had become the ruler of Atarneus and Assos. Aristotle married his niece, Pythias and they had a daughter of the same name. In Assos Aristotle founded an academy, gathering around him a group of Platonic philosophers.

After three years in Assos, Aristotle moved to the island of Lesbos, about 7 miles to the south, possibly at the invitation of Theophrastus, who was later to become Aristotle's closest follower. We know that during this period Aristotle made many biological observations.

Aristotle's family was from Stagira in Macedonia in Northern Greece. His father was court doctor to the king Amyntas II, the father of Philip of Macedonia. In 343 B.C., Aristotle was invited by Philip of Macedonia to tutor his son, Alexander the Great, then aged 14. Of course, we do not know what Aristotle taught Alexander, but it must have included Homer and the art of Government. Aristotle wrote two essays on Monarchy and Colonies for Alexander. Aristotle remained in this post for some seven years, until 336 B.C when Alexander became the king of Macedonia and began his conquest of the world.

In 334 B.C. at the age of 50, Aristotle returned to Athens to establish his own school, the Lyceum, in a grove in the north of Athens. This was said to be a spot frequented by Socrates. The return to Athens marks the third and the mature period of Aristotle's intellectual life, during which most of his famous works were composed. For the most part, these works are more like collections of notes than books, and for this reason they are often difficult to understand and have generated much debate concerning their interpretation. They were not supposed to be read by the general public, but were probably written for the students and scholars of the Lyceum, who had already attended the relevant lectures. Despite this, it is from these that we know the thoughts and work of the mature Aristotle, and it is these which had a profound influence on the history of Western Europe.

The overall character of these works reflects the nature of the Lyceum itself. It must have been a hive of creative intellectual activity. The Lyceum was a center of teaching, learning and investigation. Aristotle gathered around him fellow students of nature. Every morning Aristotle and his pupils would walk up and down the gardens discussing the more abstract areas of philosophy. It is because of this walking that Aristotelian philosophers are called the Peripatetics (from the word *peripatoi* which means covered walk). In the evenings or afternoons, there would be more popular lectures.

5

A Life

The Lyceum was an incredible research institution. Aristotle's colleagues and his pupils worked as a team under his planning and coordination. The work continued after his death. It covered almost everything. Theophrastus worked on gathering the history of different areas of philosophy. Meno wrote the history of medicine. Callisthenes catalogued the winners at the Pythian games. Theophrastus complimented Aristotle's extensive research on animals with an equally extensive investigation of plants. Strato worked on dynamics and mechanics, studying the lever, the pulley and the wedge. The constitutions of Greek cities were catalogued.

Aristotle also collected hundreds of manuscripts and the Lyceum became one of the first libraries. He also gathered maps and natural objects and specimens for what was in effect one of the first museums.

The collected works of Aristotle consists in the following:

1) <u>Logic</u>:
Categories
On Interpretation
Prior Analytics
Posterior Analytics
Topics
Sophistical Refutations

2) <u>Metaphysics</u>
Metaphysics

3) <u>Natural Philosophy</u>:
Physics
Meteorology
On the Heavens
On Generation and Corruption

4) <u>On Animals</u>
History of Animals
Parts of Animals
Movement of Animals
Progression of Animals
Generation of Animals
The Nicomachean Ethics
Eudemian Ethics
The Politics
The collection of Constitutions

5) <u>On Humans</u>
De Anima
Sense and Sensibilia
On Memory
On Sleep
On Dreams
On Divination in Sleep
On Length and Shortness of Life
On Youth, Old Age and Death
On Respiration
On Breath

6) <u>Ethics and Politics</u>
Nichomachean Ethics
Eudemian Ethics
The Politics

7) <u>Aesthetics</u>
Rhetoric
Poetics

6

This is the list of Aristotle's mature works as known to us today. There are three other types of works which have not been included in this list

a) Aristotle's early works:

Diogenes Laertius (see below) lists 19 dialogues, written during the first period of Aristotle's adult life (in the Academy) and which probably reflect Plato's views. Some of the titles are: Politicus, Sophistes, Menexenus, Symposium, Grylus (on Rhetoric), Eudemus (On the Soul. For these we have fragments. There are others for which we only have the names: On Justice, On the Poets, On Wealth, On Prayer, On Good Birth, On Education, On Pleasure, the Nerinthus and the Eroticus.

Cicero praised Aristotle's dialogues for their style. They were considered to be the equal to Plato's own dialogues, and it is for the dialogues that Aristotle was famous during antiquity. The works that we know him by were unknown outside the Lyceum.

b) Works not by Aristotle:

There are several books which are probably not by Aristotle, but which have been included in the general collection of his works. It is worth listing these, not only for the sake of clarity, but also because it gives us an idea of the breadth of the work of the Lyceum and hence of Aristotle's own interests. This grouping includes: On the Universe, On Colors, On Things Heard, Physiognomonics, On Plants, On Marvelous Things Heard, Mechanics, Problems, On Indivisible Lines, The Situation and Names of Winds, On Melisssus, Xenophanes and Gorgias, Magna Moralia, On Virtues and Vices, Economics, Rhetoric to Alexander.

c) The missing works from the mature period:

Three lists of Aristotle's works from antiquity exist. The oldest is that of Diogenes Laertius, early third century A.D (from *The Lives of the Philosophers*, v, 22-27). Earlier lists have not survived. Diogenes cites over 150 titles, and the catalogue does not include some of Aristotle's important works which have actually survived. Since we now have 32 works by Aristotle (as listed above), we might be tempted to conclude that only a fifth of Aristotle's works still exist.

This would be premature. After 322 B.C., Aristotle's library at the Lyceum was under the charge of Theophrastus. When he died, his nephew Neleus took the main works to Scepsis in Asia Minor, where he hid them in a cave. The story says that they remained there for 200 years, after which they were transferred to Rome and given to the Aristotelian philosopher, Andronicus of Rhodes, the last head of the Lyceum. Andronicus edited the manuscripts, grouping together the works according to their relevant subjects in about 60 BC. Many of Aristotle's works as known today are compilations made from shorter pieces. We only possess less than a third of Aristotle's total work.

These lists can be taken as definitive. Parts of the *Eudemian Ethics* may well have been written before Aristotle returned to Athens in 334 B.C. The same is true of parts of the *Metaphysics* and parts of his works on logic. Dating Aristotle's work is notoriously difficult; there is no firm evidence. With some works it is even unclear whether they were written by Aristotle or not. For instance, some scholars argue that the *Magna Moralia* was written by Aristotle; others not.

From the titles of the works, we can see that Aristotle's interests ranged over almost all areas of human knowledge. Given his incredible powers of observation, classification, and deduction, it is not surprising that later generations thought of him as a superman.

In June 323 B.C. Alexander died. Athens became a center of anti Macedonian feelings, and of course, Aristotle become a target for those sentiments. A charge of impiety was brought against him, based on a hymn and an epitaph that he written for Hymias. He decided to leave, probably to avoid a repetition of the fate of Socrates, "in order that the Athenians might not commit a second crime against Philosophy." He handed the direction of the Lyceum over to Theophrastus, and left for Chalcis, a Macedonian stronghold, on the island of Euboea. A year later he died. He was sixty-two.

Aristotle left a will. In it he asks to buried next to his wife Pythias, who had died several years before. He also provides his new wife, Herpyllis, who was possibly the mother of his son, Nicomachus, after whom the famous work on ethics is named.

Although there is much dispute about the chronology of Aristotle's works, there is general agreement about the direction of his intellectual development. As Ross says:

> The general movement was from otherworldliness towards an intense interest in the concrete facts of both of nature and of history, and a conviction that the `form' and meaning of the world is to be found not apart from but embodied in its matter.

3
The Nature of Investigation

In AD 529 the Emperor Justinian closed the academies of philosophy in Athens. From then on, Aristotle's thought was largely lost to Western civilization until the twelfth century, except in Constantinople. From there it passed to the Arab world. The culmination of this process was the work of Averroes, who wrote expositions on almost all of the texts of Aristotle that we now possess. He claimed that Aristotle discovered and almost perfected the three main branches of knowledge: logic, natural science and metaphysics.

Through the contact between the Europeans and Arabs in centers of learning in Spain and Sicily, Aristotle's works were translated into Latin, and gradually became known by learned people throughout Europe. In a way they caused a revolution. Knowledge of Greek thought had been largely confined to Plato, whose work was often mystical and other worldly. In contrast, Aristotle's work displayed great knowledge of the Earth, of animals, of physics and all natural phenomena.

More than anything, the book which fueled this revolution of thought was *the Organon*, a compilation of Aristotle's work on investigation and logic. This compilation covers most matters concerning empirical study, deduction and argumentation. It consists of

1) *Categories* : which concerns the basic types of words, which are the parts of complete statements

9

2) *De Interpretatione* . which is about whole statements. which form part of syllogisms
3) *Prior Analytics,* which concerns logic, the working of syllogisms
4) *Posterior Analytics:* which is about the use of syllogisms in scientific investigation
5) *Topics* in which Aristotle systematizes the dialectical use of arguments
6) *Sophistical Refutations* in which Aristotle presents the informal fallacies

Presented in this way. the compilation has an order. In it Aristotle's achievement is so huge, it is hard for us to appreciate it. In the *Sophistical Refutations* he himself writes:

> Of our present subject, however, it would not be true to say that part had already been worked out and part had not; it did not exist at all (183b34)

What he says here about informal logical fallacies and the syllogism can be extended to the whole idea of the systematic scientific investigation of nature. Not only did he and others in the Lyceum carry out such research, but Aristotle explained the methodology of these investigations. In other words, he practiced science, but he also preached a philosophy of science. Moreover. his thorough explanation of the methods of investigation served as a definitive text until the scientific revolution of the sixteenth century.

The Categories

The word 'logic' did not exist in Aristotle's time. Greek philosophers co-opted the word 'dialectic'. which normally meant 'conversation'. to refer to the process of clarifying thought and critically examining key terms.

The *Categories* is probably an early work. It is the basis of Aristotle's metaphysics and of his arguments against Parmenides and Plato. Parmenides claimed that everything is one and that change is an illusion. Aristotle argues against this position by showing that it is based on a misunderstanding of the word 'is' (we shall examine this in more detail in chapter 4). Similarly. Aristotle argues that Plato's theory of forms is partly a result of a confusion concerning the term 'is' (see chapter 6). These arguments are based on Aristotle's insight that the word 'is' has different uses which are reflected in the categories. The first four chapters of the work, the *Categories*, explain the general concept of a category and the remaining chapters discuss each particular category in turn. The fifth chapter concentrates on the primary category of substance.

To discuss the different ways in which things can be, Aristotle first defines synonymy, homonymy and paronymy. Two things are named synonymously when the same word is used to name them and the corresponding definition is the same. For example, man and ox are synonymous with regard to being animals. Two things are named homonously when they only have the same name in common and the corresponding definitions of the name are different. For example, in English the word 'bat' is used homonously. Two things are named paronymously when the two names do not pick out the same thing and do not have the same definition, but the one term is derived from the other. For example, the term 'grammarian' is derived from 'grammar'.

The terms 'exists', 'is' and 'be' are paronymous. Failure to recognize this led Plato and Parmenides astray, and as we shall see, the categories are like a catalogue of the paranymous uses of 'exists'. Aristotle gives us a list of ten categories. These are:

1) substance or what is it? (horse)
2) quantity or how much? (four foot)
3) quality or what kind?(white)
4) relations or in relation to what?(larger)
5) where (in the market-place)
6) when (yesterday)
7) position (is upright)
8) having (has-shoes-on)
9) doing (running)
10) being affected (being ridden)

These are basic different kinds of predicate. This list is repeated in the *Topics*. In other places, Aristotle cites 8 or 6 categories (dropping 'having' and 'position'). However, of the categories, the most fundamental is the first: substance (ousia). Aristotle argues that substances are the basic or primary constituents of reality, and this point is central to his metaphysics. This means that all the other categories indicate dependent existents. This is why in all lists substance, quality and quantity are always included. From this point we can also see that although Aristotle's list is of basic types of predicate terms (i.e. a linguistic classification), it is also a list of the different ways in which things can exist (i.e. ontological). For this reason, Aristotle can use the categories in his metaphysics by arguing that 'exists' is paranomous.

The reasoning which led Aristotle to think that the list of basic predicates is the same as that of basic type of existents is possibly as follows. If we ask what blue is, the answer is a color. If we ask what color is, the answer is a quality. However, we cannot ask for a higher classification for quality itself. For this reason it is a category. The basic predicates indicate the fundamental classes into which things fall. Therefore, they indicate fundamental types of things.

Sentences and propositions

Many distinctions, which seem commonsense to us now, were first made clear by Aristotle. For example, in *On Interpretation*, Chapter 4, he distinguishes sentences and statements. A sentence is a significant combination of words. A statement is a sentence that affirms or denies a predicate of a subject. For example, the statement 'Socrates is bald' affirms the predicate bald of the subject Socrates. Statements are true or false (or so it seems; the exception is discussed below). The important point is that not all sentences are statements. Prayers are sentences that are neither true nor false.

The Sea Battle

Section 9 of *On Interpretation* is one of Aristotle's most famous pieces of philosophy. He notes that apparently, for any statement either it or its denial must be true. This is called 'the principle of the excluded middle': for any statement p, it must be that either p or its denial is true.

Does the principle of the excluded middle apply to statements about particular future events? Aristotle thinks not. Regarding the future, he thinks that neither p nor its denial would be true now. Suppose I predict that tomorrow there will be a sea battle in the nearby straits. According to Aristotle, the prediction is neither true nor false yet. The future is yet to happen.

His argument has two parts. In the first part, Aristotle presents a piece of reasoning, according to which the future is entirely fixed because the law of excluded middle is true concerning statements about the future. In the second part, Aristotle rejects the piece of reasoning and tries to show that, to avoid the idea of a fixed future, we must abandon the law of excluded middle with regard to the future.

FIRST PART:

I predict that there will be a sea battle tomorrow. Is my prediction now true or is it false? Either way there is a problem. Necessarily, if the prediction is now true, then there will be a sea-battle tomorrow. Given that it is true now, there is no alternative. On the other hand, suppose that the prediction is already false; suppose it is false now that there will be a sea-battle tomorrow. Once again, necessarily, if my prediction is now false, then there will not be a sea battle tomorrow. Given that the prediction is now false, then there is no alternative outcome. Either way, it looks as if the future is fixed or predetermined, or that there is no possibility of chance.

This conclusion does not depend on the fact that we do not know what the future will hold. Today we are ignorant about what will happen tomorrow. This ignorance is irrelevant to the argument. Even if we are ignorant about the future, given that the above piece of reasoning is sound, the future is fixed. To be clear, the argument of the first step can be put as follows:

1) Necessarily, it is now either true or false that there will be a sea-battle tomorrow

2) If 1) is true then the future is fixed and there is no chance.

3) Therefore, the future is fixed and there is no chance

SECOND PART

Aristotle thinks that this is a logically valid argument, but he does not think that it is sound. He thinks that the first premise is false. In other words, he claims that the principle of the excluded middle is false concerning statements about the future. He argues for this conclusion in three steps.

13

First step: because there is chance and the future is not fixed, the conclusion 3) is false.

Second step: because the argument is valid, at least one of the premises must be false.

Third step: premise 2) is true, and therefore 1) must be false.

In other words, given that the future is not fixed, and given the truth of 2) (i.e. that the law of excluded middle means that it is), it follows that 1) must be false. In this way, Aristotle concludes that statements about particular future events are not true or false now. In this sense, they differ from statements about the past, which are.

The focus of debate has been the second premise. Some commentators think Aristotle's reasoning for this premise is faulty because it relies on a modal fallacy. The fallacy is to argue from:

a) Necessarily (either the Sea Battle will take place or it will not.)

to

b) Either necessarily the Sea Battle will take place or necessarily it will not:

in other words, from

a) N (Either p or not p)

to

b) Either N(p) or N(not p), where N means necessarily.

The objection is that a) does not imply b). The problem is that the law of excluded middle states a). Whereas the claim that the future is fixed requires b). Therefore, if a) does not imply b), then fatalism does not follow from the principle of the excluded middle. In which case, Aristotle cannot argue the third step above, namely that premise 2 is true.

Logic

In *the Prior Analytics* Aristotle develops his theory of the syllogism. He defines a syllogism as:

An argument in which, certain things having been taken, something other than the things taken follows necessarily by their being so.

In other words, it concerns logically valid arguments, arguments in which the conclusion follows logically from the premises. In the first chapter, Aristotle classifies the propositions that are the premises of any syllogism. As we have seen, he defines a proposition or statement as a sentence that affirms or denies a predicate of a subject. Consequently, he considers all statements to be of the subject-predicate form. He classifies them according to quantity, quality and modality. Leaving aside modality for the moment, statements are either universal or particular (their quantity) and either affirmative or negative (their quality). Consequently, there are four types of such propositions:

A Universal affirmative   All humans are mortal
E Universal negative   No humans are mortal
I Particular affirmative   Some humans are mortal
O Particular negative   Some humans are not mortal

AEIO are the letters used by the Medieval philosophers to indicate each of these kinds of statements. (In *On Interpretation* Aristotle treats singular statements about individuals, such as 'Socrates is mortal', as a third type of quantity. In the *Prior Analytics* , this type is absorbed by the second, the particular.)

Aristotle notes the logical relations between these statement-kinds:

1) **a** and **o** are contradictories and
e and **i** are contradictories.
They cannot both be true and they cannot both be false.
2) **a** and **e** are not contradictory: they are contraries.
They cannot both be true, but they could both be false.
3) **i** and **o** are sub-contraries:

They can both be true but they cannot both be false.
Concerning modality, Aristotle distinguishes three kinds of statements.

The Nature of Investigation

1) A belongs to B. (e.g. Humans are mortal)
2) A necessarily belongs to B. (e.g. Humans are necessarily mortal)
3) A may belong to B. (e.g. Humans are possibly mortal)

Aristotle develops a theory of the syllogism, to which we now turn, and the theory extends to these modal statements.

Types of Syllogism

Aristotle's aim is to determine which syllogisms are valid and which are not, and to explain why. He does not attempt to do this by making logic into an axiomatic system, as Euclid did to geometry a generation later. His perhaps more pragmatic aim is to classify syllogisms, so that they will be clear tools in making valid deductions, and to explain what their validity consists in.

All of Aristotle's syllogisms consist of three statements; they consist of two premises and a conclusion. The two premises have one term in common which is called the middle term. For example,

Argument 1
Major premise: All animals are mortal
Minor premise: All humans are animals
Conclusion: All humans are mortal

In these two premises the middle term is "animal." It appears in both premises and not in the conclusion. The major term is the predicate in the conclusion (i.e. mortal) and the minor term is the subject in the conclusion (i.e. human). The premises are named major and minor accordingly.

Aristotle uses this idea of the middle term as a basis to classify the general types of syllogisms based on the structural relations between their premises. Later this will serve as a basis to classify all the different types of valid syllogisms. At this initial stage, he does not want to take into account the different sentence types, only the structure of the syllogism itself. There are three forms of combination, which Aristotle calls the three figures.

These are:

FIRST FIGURE	SECOND FIGURE	THIRD FIGURE
Subject –Predicate	Subject–Predicate	Subject–Predicate
...Ms are A	...As are M	...Ms are A
...Cs are M	...Cs are M	...Ms are C

(M stands for the middle term). In other words, the first figure consists of a major premise in which something is predicated of the middle term and a minor premise in which the middle term is predicated of something else. Argument 1 is an example of a syllogism of the first figure.

In each of these figures, each of the two premises in question could be a statement of one of the four forms: A or E or I or O mentioned above. For example, the following would be a syllogism for the first figure with two universal affirmative premises (statements of type A):

All Greeks are animals
All Athenians are Greeks
Therefore all Athenians are animals

Aristotle then tries to prove which syllogisms of these forms would be valid and which would not. He works methodically through all 16 combinations for each one of the three figures. The method of proof he uses is as follows. Aristotle thinks that certain deductions are obvious; these he calls complete or perfect. Starting from these complete syllogisms, he uses certain rules to deduce the other valid syllogisms. The rules are:

If every S is P, then some S is P
If some S is P, then some P is S
If no S is P, then no P is S

Aristotle claims that the four complete or perfect deductions are all in first figure. They are:

Barbara	Celarent	Darii	Ferio
All Ms are A	No Bs are A	All Bs are A	No B is A
All Bs are M	All Cs are B	Some C is B	Some C is B
All Bs are A	No Cs are A	Some Cs are A	Some C is not A

17

Aristotle derives 10 other valid syllogistic forms from these, giving a total of 14 types of valid syllogism. Medieval thinkers gave each one a name. Above are the names of the four perfect syllogisms.

Deriving these valid forms from others is only part of the work. For the sake of completeness, Aristotle must also show that these 14 forms are the only valid syllogisms. He does this by argument from counter-examples, showing that other syllogistic forms are not valid because they might have true premises and a false conclusion.

In his discussions of each figure, Aristotle arrives at some general conclusions about the valid form in each of the figures. For instance, only in the first figure can universal affirmative conclusions be reached. In the second figure, only negative conclusions can be established and in the third, only particular.

Perhaps Aristotle's main achievement in logic was that he was the first person to use symbols to stand for words in an argument. This is a simple but deep insight, because it amounts to seeing that the validity of an argument depends on its logical form and not on its content. Aristotle's logical theory is remarkably systematic. His theory, however, is not complete. In particular, Aristotle did not see that there is a branch of logic which concerns the logical connections between whole propositions, what we now call propositional logic. Specifically, there are inference patterns governed by the terms 'or', 'and' 'if.. then' and 'not'. For example, if P then Q entails if not-Q then not-P.

The Scientific Method

In book I of the *Posterior Analytics* Aristotle develops his theory of demonstration, which is the use of syllogisms in gaining knowledge. Aristotle does not affirm that all propositions can be demonstrated. He admits that conclusions can be demonstrated from premises which themselves cannot be demonstrated and yet can be known. He divides the starting points or basic premises of any demonstration into three kinds: axioms, definitions and hypotheses. Axioms are principles without which reasoning would be impossible. For example, the law of excluded middle says that any predicate must either be truly affirmed or truly denied of any subject. Definitions state the meaning of the terms. A hypothesis is an assumption about what exists. For example, in geometry we assume points and lines exist.

Aristotle thinks that scientific demonstration must meet certain conditions. He thinks scientific explanation must take the form of a conclusion explained by various premises, from which it (the conclusion) follows logically. (This is similar to the twentieth century idea of deductive-nomological explanation according to which the combined statements of a cause, of the relevant causal laws and of the initial conditions should entail the effect).

Secondly, this is not enough. To be scientific, the premises of the deductive argument must have certain characteristics. They must be

> True and primitive and immediate and more familiar than and prior to and explanatory of the conclusion. (Post.An I.2.71b22)

According to Aristotle, if the premises of an argument do not satisfy these conditions, we should not call the syllogism a scientific demonstration. Aristotle gives the example of the nearness of the planet. Suppose the planets do not twinkle because they are so close to the Earth. Given all this the following would be a valid syllogism with true premises (a sound syllogism):

Argument C
1. Planets do not twinkle;
2. All heavenly bodies which do not twinkle are near;
3. Therefore the planets are near

For Aristotle, despite the fact that this syllogism is sound, it does not constitute a scientific demonstration, because it does not explain. The conclusion 3 is not explained by the premises 1 and 2. Their not twinkling does not explain why the planets are near (it is rather the other way around). Consequently, argument C is merely 'a syllogism of the that' and it is not 'a syllogism of the because.' In contrast, the planets do not twinkle because they are so near. So argument D is a syllogism in which the conclusion is explained by the premises.

Argument D
1. The planets are near;
2. All heavenly bodies which are near do not twinkle
3. Therefore the planets do not twinkle

Thirdly, Aristotle places further restrictions on what counts as a scientific demonstration. He claims that the premises themselves must be necessary truths.

> Demonstrative knowledge comes from necessary starting
> points – for what is known cannot be otherwise.(Post. An.
> I.6.74b5)

Aristotle is perhaps right to insist that scientific demonstration must show what could not be otherwise. To thoroughly explain an event, we must show why it had to happen, given all the causal conditions. Otherwise, there would be some aspect of the event which had not been explained. However, even if an explanation must show why the event had to have happened given all the causal factors, this does not mean that those causal factors are necessary themselves. Why does he say that they are?

To explain this doubt in today's terms: The starting points of a scientific explanation must include some relevant causal laws which perhaps could be considered as necessary truths. However they would also have to include a statement of the cause and initial conditions (such as the force with which the projectile was launched and a statement specifying the force of gravity). The latter statements do not seem to be necessary truths. Aristotle himself seems to acknowledge this:

> It is obvious that if the propositions from which a syllogism
> are derived are universal, the conclusion of such a
> demonstration must itself be an eternal truth too. So there can
> be no demonstration of perishable things, nor scientific
> knowledge of them strictly speaking, since the attribute does
> not hold of the thing universally, but at some time and in
> some way (Post. An. I.8.75b21)

Aristotle's claim that the premises must be necessary seems to remove the empirical and contingent elements from scientific demonstration. It restricts science to necessary truths. This seems to contradict Aristotle's own method of work, for he was a very keen observer of nature. Aristotle represents a turning point in the history of science precisely because he appreciated the importance of detailed empirical investigation. How, then, do we explain Aristotle's claim that scientific demonstrations must begin from necessary starting points?

Part of the explanation is that we should not assume that the equivalent Greek word really corresponds to what we mean now by 'science'. Today we think of the natural sciences as the systematic empirical investigation of nature. Aristotle may have meant something more akin to the pursuit of knowledge which is certain and universal.

Definitions

We can explain the discrepancy between Aristotle's theory and his practice also partly in terms of his views concerning the role of definitions in science. These are stated in chapter II of the *Posterior Analytics*. As we shall see later, natural kinds form a central part of Aristotle's metaphysics. In some sense, according to Aristotle, reality consists primarily of natural kinds of objects, such as individual plants and animals of different species. The natural kinds have a real essence (without which they would not be what they are). For example, the real essence of a human being is to be rational. Based on these real essences, there are real definitions of each natural kind; for example, by definition humans are rational animals. These real definitions have an important role in science, because explanations must start from them.

Induction

Most of the *Posterior Analytics* is dedicated to the nature of demonstration based on universal principles. Towards the end of the book (book II chapter 19), Aristotle asks how we know these universal principles. He rejects the claim that such knowledge is innate on the grounds that it is difficult to suppose that we have such knowledge without supposing that we know that we have it.

The only alternative seems to be that we acquire such knowledge through sense-perception. Aristotle agrees with this arguing that we ascend from particular sense experiences to knowledge of universal statements by induction. He contrasts deduction with induction. The deductive syllogistic reasoning explained above can give us knowledge of particulars from that of universals. Induction is necessary to obtain knowledge of universals from that of particulars. Aristotle recognizes that it is by induction that we gain the knowledge for the axioms, definitions and hypotheses on which deduction is based.

Nevertheless, in the *Prior Analytics* he claims that the perfect type of induction would be a form of deductive syllogism. This perfect induction would be possible when we know all the particulars of a class. To adapt his own example, if man, horse, ass, ... are long-lived and if man, horse, ass ... are without bile, and only those animals listed are bileless, then we can conclude that all bileless animals are long lived.

To conclude, Aristotle believes that knowledge is derived from sense-perception and induction. About the life of bees, he writes:

> This, then, seems to be what happens with regard to the generation of bees...However, the facts have not been sufficiently ascertained. And if they are ever ascertained, then we must trust the evidence of the senses rather than theories, and theories as well, so long as their results agree with what is observed. (760b27)

Dialectic

Dialectic is the art of systematic discussion and of using deduction from reputable opinion. Aristotle's work on dialectic is contained in the *Topics* and the *Sophistical Refutations.* The aim of the*Topics* is to:

> Find a method by which we shall be able to argue about any proposed problem from probable premises and shall ourselves under examination avoid self-contradiction. (100 a 20)

The word `probable' signals a contrast with scientific syllogisms, which have immediate and certain premises. The dialectical syllogism has premises which are reasonable in the sense that they commend themselves `as probable` to most people.

For Aristotle, dialectic is an important tool of enquiry. First, it deals with claims which we do not know for certain, but which are probable. Because of this, it is useful. For example, when discussing the nature of reality, Aristotle uses the conclusions of earlier philosophers as a starting point for his own investigation. He looks to see what these views have in common and uses that as a base. Also, sometimes he appeals to what is commonly held. Also, Aristotle sometimes tries to discover what is true in the philosophical views he opposes. These are all hall-marks of Aristotle's pragmatic or commonsense approach to knowledge.

Second, the dialectical method is necessary for finding first or fundamental principles. In this way it is part of the philosophical method. These first principles have a very important role in knowledge for Aristotle. Real understanding requires appeal to causes and, ultimately, first principles.

The *Topics* is like a catalogue of advice concerning the art of arguing. It focuses on different kinds of conclusions, definitions, and commonplace rules for arguing in ethics, or regarding species, and for the arrangement of questions. For example:

> it is a good rule also, occasionally to bring an objection
> against oneself; for answerers are put off their guard against
> those who appear to be arguing impartially. It is useful too,
> too add that so and so is generally held; for people are shy of
> upsetting the received opinion. (VIII 156b 18)

In the *Sophistical Refutations* Aristotle classifies common fallacies in argument. There are two kinds; those based on language and those which are not. Among those which do, there are:

Equivocation- when a single word is ambiguous
Amphiboly- when the structure of a sentence is ambiguous

Among the fallacies which are not linguistic, Aristotle identifies the begging the question – illicitly assuming what you set out to prove, and the false dichotomy- offering your opponent only two alternatives when there are others, such as (as we have seen) 'to be or not to be.'

4

Physics

Parmenides, born in 515 B.C, denied the existence of time. He claimed that there is only one thing. It is an indivisible whole. It is non-temporal and unchangeable. He rejected the evidence of the senses, which according to him, gives us the illusion of change and of being separate from the One Being. He tried to prove his view by reasoning. His argument against change is surprisingly simple. All thought must be about something. Consequently, it is impossible to think about and study something which does not exist. It is impossible to think about nothing. Consequently, it is impossible to say of something that it no longer exists. All change requires that something goes out of existence, and therefore change is impossible.

Parmenides is backed by even more powerful arguments, known as Zeno's Paradoxes. Zeno was a follower of Parmenides, and what we call his paradoxes were in fact arguments to demonstrate the truth of his master's teaching. Supported by such powerful arguments, Parmenides' views became popular in Greece.

These views contradict the very basis of Aristotle's philosophy, even his classification of knowledge. He divides knowledge into the theoretical, the practical and the productive; the first is concerned with understanding for its own sake; the second with the good, and the third with the beautiful. Theoretical knowledge is divided into the physics, mathematics and theology. Physics deals with things which have a separate existence and which change; mathematics with things which do not change and do not have a separate existence. Theology

24

concerns that which has a separate existence and does not change (i.e. God).

Aristotle's works on nature are about things which change. The book the *Physics* deals with the fundamental general principles of nature. His other works concern more specific aspects of nature, the movement of the stars, the elements and coming to be and passing away. In this chapter, we will concentrate on the more abstract and philosophical work in physics; in the next, we will briefly examine his view of nature.

The important point is that, for Aristotle, nature essentially involves change. 'Physics' means nature and nature is the totality of natural objects, things which are subject to change. Understanding nature requires us to grasp the principles of natural change.

In book 1 of the *Physics*, Aristotle sets out to show why the views of Parmenides are mistaken. He argues that there is a confusion about change inherent in his views. Aristotle's diagnosis of change leads him to formulate the form/matter distinction, which is the core of his metaphysics and philosophy of mind. To refute Zeno's arguments against change, he develops a theory of the infinite, which we will look at later in this chapter.

Change

To arrive at basic principles for understanding nature and change, Aristotle reviews earlier Greek schools of thought. He notes that they all recognize contraries (such as solid and void, up and down) as among the first principles. Aristotle agrees with this idea because of what first principles are: like contraries, they cannot be generated from one another, otherwise they would not be first. Furthermore, all other things must be generated from the first principles.

Without discussing what the primary principles of nature actually are, Aristotle argues that there must be at least two because they must involve contraries. He then notes that contraries are adjectival. Consequently, they presuppose a substance, or rather matter, in which they inhere. Consequently, there are three basic principles of natural change: matter, and two contraries. In other words, all change involves three elements: the thing which changes; how it was before and how it is after the change. Aristotle concludes that change requires the ideas of opposites and something underlying the alteration.

In chapter seven of book 1, he argues that there are two kinds of change. He distinguishes:

X comes to be Y
Y comes to be from X

The first are alterations in a substance. A person learns music. She becomes musical. She changes from being unmusical to being musical. Such alterations involve three elements: the person, musical and unmusical.

The second kind of change involves the coming into being of a new thing. These changes are called substantial generation. Unlike alterations, this second kind of change does not involve a new condition of a pre-existing thing. It involves the generation of a new thing. Aristotle claims that only substances can go through this second kind of change. They come into being by having form imposed on matter. For example, a statue comes into being when bronze is given a form. This kind of change requires the form/matter distinction.

Aristotle uses his account of the two kinds of change to argue against Parmenides, who thought that being could not come from not-being, and hence, that change is impossible. Aristotle's reply is that Parmenides' view is too simplistic.

Do alterations (first kind of change) involve being coming from not-being? When it is described in terms of the quality, the change appears to begin from what is not: (the musical comes from what is not musical). However, when the alteration is described in terms of substance, the starting point of change is what is (i.e. the person, who becomes musical). So, in this case, Parmenides is mistaken.

Does substantial generation (the second type of change) require being coming from not being? Aristotle's reply is the same as before. The change can be described so that it appears as if something comes from nothing. However, the change can also be described to show that it does not. In the second type of change a new substance or thing comes into being. For example, a baby is born. This looks like something from nothing. Nevertheless, through such changes something permanent persists: matter. The matter acquires a new form, and becomes a thing which previously did not exist. So, in this case too, Parmenides is mistaken.

To make the point more clear, Aristotle introduces the distinction between actual and potential. According to him, all change involves the turning of something potential into something actual. When a person becomes musical, they were potentially musical before, and this potential becomes actual. Similarly, the seed is potentially a tree. Both kinds of change involve the potential becoming actual, and it is this aspect of change that Parmenides fails to take into account. What Parmenides would call 'not-being' is really potentially being. In this way, by analyzing the two kinds of change, Aristotle introduces his form-matter distinction to show us why Parmenides is mistaken.

Form and matter are not two independently existing things. They are two aspects of any substance or thing, which are only separable in thought. This distances him from Plato, who conceived of the Forms as independently existing universals.

Exactly how we should understand the form/matter distinction is the subject of chapter six. However, initially, we can conceive of form as the structure or organization of a natural thing. For example, the form of an animal is the way the matter of its body is organized such that it has the power to grow, perceive and move in the way it does. This is the essence of the animal, and this nature defines its power of movement. The matter is the material out of which the substance or thing in question is composed. Matter cannot exist without form and form requires matter. They are two aspects of any particular thing.

This distinction can be drawn at different levels. The body is the matter of a person. Flesh is the matter of a body. The matter of any compound will be one or more of the four elements, fire, air, earth water. The form/matter distinction can be applied to the elements themselves.

Aristotle does not think that physics should only study matter. It is the study of nature, and as such, it should study the nature of things, which means their form. Their form defines their development, the direction in which they change. Furthermore, Aristotle thinks that sometimes parts can only be understood in terms of the whole. In short, physics requires us to understand nature, and this requires us to be able to explain, and not all explanation concerns the material.

The Four Causes

To understand things in physics, we must know how to explain them. To this end, Aristotle distinguishes four different kinds of causes, or rather ways of explaining things.

The material cause:
The word 'cause' can be applied to 'that out of which a thing comes to be and which is present as a constituent in the product'. We can explain by citing what the thing is made of. For example, the fact that a sphere is made of bronze explains many of its other properties.

The formal cause:
'Cause' is also applied to the form or 'the formula of what it is to be the thing in question.' We can explain by citing the essence of the thing. For example, we explain many things that people do by citing the fact that to be human is to be a certain kind of animal. By specifying what something is, we can explain why it does what it does.

The efficient cause:
This is that 'from which comes the immediate origin of the movement or rest.' For example, a person constructing is the cause of a building. Or, his throwing is the cause of the window breaking.

The final cause:
A cause can also be the end or aim of the thing in question. We can explain by specifying why something is done. For example, we can explain artifacts in terms of the purpose for which they were made. We can explain organs or the parts of plants in terms of their usefulness.

It is best to think of these causes as different types of explanation. For the most part, Aristotle thinks that things have all four types of cause or explanation. There are exceptions: although eyes serve a purpose; eye color does not, and cannot be explained by citing a final cause. Furthermore, the same thing can serve as more than one type of cause. In particular, the form can also serve as the final cause (see below). Despite the exceptions, in investigating nature, we should seek all four kinds of cause. This means that, for Aristotle, natural things have final causes or ends. This claim seems alien to us who think of nature and its diverse forms as the result only of physical laws, without reference to ends. In book II.8 of the *Physics*, Aristotle argues against a purely mechanistic view of nature on the following grounds:

Natural changes occur in a very regular way.
By definition, things which happen by chance involve a lack of regularity.
What does not happen by chance must happen for a purpose.
Therefore, natural changes happen for a purpose

Of course, the weakness in this argument is the third premise which does not consider the alternative that things can happen regularly because of natural causal laws. Aristotle also argues that nature is analogous to human art. Probably at the root of both of these arguments is that any purely mechanical or material explanation of things would be insufficient to explain the form.

Aristotle's view is not that stones have desires. It is rather that all natural things have a nature, which is their form, according to which they tend to develop. This natural development is an end. Therefore, we can explain the growth of a tree teleologically, in terms of the end of its nature, without affirming that it desires. This teleological explanation is at the same time a formal explanation, because it requires the idea of the form of the tree. Aristotle thinks that the same kind of explanations can be extended to inanimate things, as we shall now see.

Movement

Galileo promoted two major changes in our conception of the world. In 1632 he published the *Dialogue concerning the Two Chief World Systems-Ptolemaic and Copernican*. In this, he argued that the Earth revolves around the Sun. In 1638 he published the *Discourse concerning Two New Sciences*, part of which argues for the principle of inertia. Inertia implies that a body moving in vacuum will continue its movement indefinitely, unless acted on by some resisting force. Inertia is a very important concept in the development of physics. It implies that force is required to bring about changes in velocity (rather than to just maintain existing velocity). Without it, Newton could not have formulated his laws of motion.

These two points in Galileo's science mark the end of Aristotle's domination in physics (in astronomy and dynamics). What is remarkable about both is that, initially, one might think that observation favors Aristotle, as against Galileo. We do not feel the Earth move; so it seems reasonable to conclude that the Earth is at rest and that the sun is moving. And, if you do not continue to push them, bodies always come to a rest. The vindication of Galileo and the fall of Aristotle lies in more sophisticated observations.

According to Aristotle, force is necessary to maintain a body in motion and Medieval thinkers followed him on this point, as on many others. He claims that a body can only move when it is in contact with the mover. He realizes that this presents a problem regarding projectiles. You throw a stone, and it continues to move after you have let it go. According to Aristotle, it continues because of the effect of the movement on the air particles. The power of movement is communicated through those particles. However, this power decreases as the distance from the mover increases, and the stone will come to rest, quite independently of any opposing forces or resistance.

Aristotle thinks that all change must be initiated by the action of an external body. For example, someone makes a hole in a bucket and the water pours out. However, he also thinks that all natural objects have an inner tendency to movement, without which they would not move. This applies to natural inanimate objects as well as to living things. This is part of what it means for them to be natural – they have a natural tendency to move. Aristotle thinks that the four elements have a natural place: fire moves up; and earth moves down; each will come to rest in their natural place. It is their nature to move so. Artifacts only have this tendency because of their matter, the material out of which they are composed, and not because of their form. In summary, both the inner (the form and the end) and outer (the impulse or external force) components are necessary for change. Aristotle says that inanimate things have in themselves "a beginning of being moved" but not "a beginning of causing movement."

Place and time are both presuppositions of movement. The existence of place is shown by the fact that movement involves displacement. For example, water moves in and displaces the air. Such displacement presupposes space. Place is the limit within which a body exists. Interestingly, Aristotle realizes that this means that, although everything in the universe has a place, the universe as a whole does not. Thus, the only way to suppose that the universe moves is that it turns.

Time and the Infinite

Time is puzzling. Aristotle sees that time is linked to motion. However, the two cannot be identified, because there are many movements, but only one time. Only things which could be in motion can be in time. Things which are eternal and immobile are not. Aristotle uses this point to argue that time itself is eternal – it never began, and will never end. This conclusion is important for Aristotle in establishing the nature of the unmoved mover in the *Metaphysics*. (see below).

One of the puzzles about time, for Aristotle, is that it is counted but it is also a continuum. He defines time as that aspect of movement which is counted. He means that, in movement, we can recognize a plurality of phases. Counting seems to require the idea of discrete units. However, Aristotle also maintains that time is a continuum, which implies that it is not discrete. Time seems to have contradictory properties.

The solution of this old puzzle is pivotal for Aristotle's work. Solving it requires him to answer Zeno's Paradoxes, and doing that will help him refute the position of Parmenides.

The Infinite

Aristotle claims that an infinite body is impossible. Every body must be bounded by a surface, and no infinite body could be so bounded. He also argues that an actual infinite body could neither be a simple nor a composite. Therefore such a thing cannot exist.

However, he recognizes the need for a concept of the infinite in mathematics. The series of natural numbers is infinite, for example. He introduces the important distinction between the actually infinite and the potentially infinite. He denies the existence of the actual infinite. Therefore, as a continuum, a line does not consist in an infinite number of actual points. It can be divided indefinitely, but such a division could never realized in actuality. Therefore, the line is only potentially infinite.

Similarly, time is only potentially infinite. It can be added to indefinitely. There is no last event. Furthermore, we can go back in time indefinitely. There is no first event. However, these two points do not make time an actual infinity, because successive moments do not co-exist. For Aristotle, the nature of time is defined by now, or the present moment, as being what exists. It is only in relation to the now that we can specify past and future. Different times do not co-exist at the same time. Therefore, time itself is not an actual infinity. Its infinite nature is merely potential: for any moment, it is possible to find an earlier and later moment.

In his denial of the actual infinite, Aristotle reverses the traditional view of infinity. We tend to think of the infinite as that

Physics

which contains everything, as something complete. On the contrary, says Aristotle, the infinite is something which is never complete.

Zeno's Paradoxes

These are not really paradoxes. A paradox is an apparently inescapable contradiction. Zeno does not see a contradiction; he smells an argument. Zeno's so-called 'paradoxes' are really arguments, designed to prove the startling conclusion that motion is not possible, in order to support Parmenides' claim that the universe is one whole, indivisible and unchanging thing.

Zeno states four arguments for his conclusion (the mid-way problem, Achilles; the arrow; and the stadium). These arguments are known through Aristotle's exposition and criticisms of them, in the *Physics* book V, 9. Despite their important differences, the four arguments have a similar form, and we shall concentrate on the mid-way problem and the arrow.

THE MIDWAY PROBLEM

Imagine that you have to cross a room, by travelling half of the distance across it, then half of the remaining distance and half of the remaining distance and so on. You will never actually cross the room. The journey cannot be completed. However, the same is true of any journey, and therefore no journey or movement can even begin.

The form of this argument is:
For anything to move requires its completing an infinite number of tasks.
It is impossible to complete an infinite number of tasks.
Therefore, movement is impossible.

In the first premise moving requires an infinite number of tasks because space is continuous, and hence infinitely divisible. This means that between any two points, there are an infinite number of points. This in turn implies that to move between any two points requires completing an infinite number of steps or tasks.

In the second premise sometimes it seems that Zeno's point is that it is impossible to complete an infinite number of tasks in a finite time. However, his real point is that it is impossible to complete an infinite series because an infinite series has no last member.

This is Zeno's argument. In reply, effectively, Aristotle rejects the notion of an infinite number of tasks. A line does not consist in an actual infinite number of points; a line is a continuum which can be divided indefinitely. Therefore, in relation to the first premise, for something to move does not require it completing an actual infinite number of real tasks. Rather, the distance moved can be divided indefinitely.

THE ARROW

Imagine an arrow flying through space. Zeno argues:

At any moment, the arrow occupies a space which is equal to its own size.
Something which occupies a space equal to its own size is at rest.
Therefore, at any moment, the arrow is at rest.

This conclusion can be generalized to show that no motion is possible.

Aristotle's reply is:

> Time is not composed of indivisible nows any more than any other magnitude is composed of indivisibles. (Phy VI.9. 239b8)

In other words, he rejects the very idea of something being either at rest or in motion at an instant. The first premise of the above argument is therefore based on a mistake, because of the phrase 'at any moment'. A period of time does not consist of an actual infinity of instants or nows, just as a line does not consist in an actual infinity of points. A period of time can be divided indefinitely, but this makes a potential infinity and not an actual one.

First cause; no first event

In *Physics* VIII. Aristotle argues that there must be a first cause of all change which is itself eternal and changeless. Motion has no beginning in time, but nevertheless, there must be source of movement in the universe as a whole. There is a first cause, but no first event.

Aristotle tries to establish that change has always been happening and always will. In effect, he argues that there is no first change. This he thinks follows from his definition of change, and also from the commonsense claim that any change presupposes the existence of things capable of changing.

His first argument is that every change must have an explanation. However, this explanation must always refer to a previous event. To explain how things (that are capable of change) come into being, we must assume some other previous change. Otherwise there would be nothing to explain in terms of or with. Consequently, any change requires an explanation of why it happened, and this explanation must refer to a previous event. Consequently, there cannot be a first event.

Aristotle presents us with another argument to the same conclusion. This is based on the nature of time. Time itself cannot start or end. It is eternal. However, time is just the possibility of change. Therefore, change itself cannot have begun and cannot end, just like time. There is no first event.

In *Physics* (book VIII) Aristotle establishes the need for an unmoved mover or for a first cause with the following argument: At each instant, all movement requires a mover. Whatever is moved must be moved by something else. But, the primary cause of movement in the universe could not be a moved mover, because this would lead to an infinite regress. Therefore, there must be an unmoved mover.

In the *Metaphysics*, Aristotle claims that the unmoved mover must be actual. All movement implies potentiality, but the cause of the movement must be something actual. For example, to heat something, one must use something which is already hot. We can generalize this to the claim the actualization of something potential must be caused by something which is itself actual. In this way, he tries to establish the unmoved mover must be something which is completely actual. This is a first step to showing that the unmoved mover should be called God.

5
NATURE

The Superlunary World

According to Aristotle, the universe consists of two worlds – the superlunary and the sublunary. The superlunary world begins at the moon, going upwards, and it consists of the stars and planets. The stars are in an eternal, constant circular motion and they are otherwise unchanging, which is why they are called the fixed stars. Aristotle argues that the stars are made of a fifth element, which moves naturally in a circle. Aristotle called this element which is additional to traditional four, the first element, because he thought of it as divine. Later writers called it the aether.

These claims were based on the belief that observations over generations had shown that the stars move in constant circles. Given that, Aristotle has to explain their motion. He tries to do so in *On the Heavens.* The theory of motion which best fits the empirical evidence of the time suggested that the four elements (earth, water, fire and air) move naturally in straight line. Other non-rectilinear movements require some intervention, as was explained in the previous chapter. Therefore, to explain the ever constant, circular movement of the stars required the postulation of the fifth element. Consequently, according to Aristotle. the division between the two worlds was necessary primarily to account for observations.

Furthermore, Aristotle knew that the distance between the Earth and the stars was very great. He theorized that if this space was filled with one of the four sublunary elements, say air, then there would be an imbalance between the qualities of hot and cold, and wet and dry in the universe (Met 340a1). He concluded that this space could not be filled with one of the four sublunary elements. Since there is no void, there must be another element. Aristotle thought that his theory agreed with aspects of traditional religious belief of the time. (Cael 270b5)

The unmoved movers

As we saw in the previous chapter. Aristotle argues for the existence of an unmoved mover. Without it motion could not be explained. In chapter 8 of the *Physics*, Aristotle discusses the number of unmoved movers. The constant circular motion of the outermost "fixed" stars is simple compared to the sometimes irregular and complex motion of the planets, the Sun and the Moon. How should this irregular motion be explained?

Earlier, in Plato's Academy, Eudoxus had tried to solve the problem by postulating a number of concentric spheres, inclined at slightly different angles, and rotating at different speeds. He postulated four spheres for each of the four known planets and, three each for the Sun and Moon. In this way, he was able to explain a huge amount of observational detail, including the rotation of the Sun and the Moon, and the mentioned irregularities. This mathematical model was refined by Aristotle's friend, Callippus.

Aristotle tried to explain how this theoretical model would work in practice, that is how movement could be transferred mechanically from the outermost sphere to the sublunary world. To do this, and for reasons concerning interference between the spheres which we will not go into, he had to postulate 55 spheres. Although he does so tentatively and undogmatically, this result is based on trying to make the mathematical model of Eudoxus (as amended by Callippus) work in practice. Hence, apparently, Aristotle thinks that there are fifty-five unmoved movers, each one moving a sphere. For reasons which will become clear in the next chapter, Aristotle apparently thought of these unmoved movers as non-material intelligent beings, which are inferior to the prime mover, God (see the next chapter).

The Sublunary World

The sublunary world, below the moon, is one of change and decay,. According to Aristotle, the Earth is a sphere, which is at rest in the center of the universe. The earth is stationary; the heavens move around it. Around the Earth, below the moon, lies concentric, layers or spheres of water, air and fire.

Aristotle distinguished natural and forced movements. Without intervention, earth will fall downwards, in a straight line towards the center of the universe. Without intervention, fire will rise upwards, away from the center of the universe. In this way, each of the elements has its own proper or natural position or place. The remaining two elements are intermediary in terms of their natural position.

These points also help us understand part of Aristotle's resistance to the idea of an infinite universe. All natural movements must come to completion, an end. This requires the idea of a natural place for the elements. However, the idea of a natural place does not make sense in an infinitely large universe that has no center and no extreme ends. Furthermore, according to Aristotle, in an infinite universe, there could be no distinction between heavy and light because this depends on the idea of a natural resting place. (Physics 3,5,205a19-20)

Although Aristotle's account seems strange to us, it is a remarkably commonsensical theory which has some support in empirical observation. For example, the Earth appears to be stationary. For instance, Aristotle's idea that earth (the element) has a natural tendency to move downwards has some basis in observation- that is what we see. Less obviously, his claim that the Earth is spherical is based on the fact that the eclipses of the moon show a curved outline of the Earth. He also observed that the visible position of stars on the horizon changes slightly with the observer's position. From this he concluded that the Earth was convex and hence spherical. (Cael. 297b30) According to Aristotle, the circumference of the Earth is equivalent to 46,000 miles; the real figure is just under 25,000. We do not know the method by which this relatively prediction was obtained.

The Four Elements

In his *Meteorology*, Aristotle refines his theory of the four elements. He postulates four principles: hot, cold, dry and wet. He then explains the four elements in terms of the combination of these four basic powers. Earth is cold and dry; water is cold and wet. Air is hot and wet and fire is hot and dry. He then uses these to explain other physical properties, such as weight, roughness, and malleability. For example, brittleness can be reduced to dryness. Softness can be reduced to the wet and hardness to the dry. The theory also seems to explain various physical changes. For example, when water boils, it changes from the wet and cold (water) to the wet and hot (air). In other words, the cold becomes hot.

The theory of the four elements was derived from Empedocles. The competing theory of the time was that of the Atomists, especially Democritus, who claimed that the physical universe consists of fundamental particles, whose differences in shape, position and arrangement underlies all the other physical differences. Aristotle opposed the Atomist theory on the grounds that matter is a continuum, like space itself. According to Aristotle, there are no ultimate, indivisible particles.

Aristotle says that atomism was motivated by an argument based on Zeno's Paradoxes (De Gen. 1.2, 316a11). According to this argument for atomism, matter could not be infinitely divisible without generating a contradiction. For, suppose an infinite division of matter were completed. In which case, what would one be left with? Either there would be parts with no magnitude, or nothing, or parts with an indivisible magnitude. The first two options are absurd, because something without a magnitude could constitute something with a magnitude. And the third option contradicts the claim that matter is infinitely divisible. Hence, there are indivisible atoms.

Aristotle replies to this argument making essentially the same point that he does in refuting Zeno's Paradoxes. He claims that to reject the idea of indivisible atoms does not require one to accept the idea of actual infinity of parts. Potentially, matter is infinitely divisible, and for this reason, there are no basic atoms. The claim that matter is a potential infinity does not mean that it is an actual infinite collection of parts. The division of matter can never be completed.

From Matter to Parts

The sublunary world is made up of the four elements. In *On Generation and Corruption*, Aristotle tries to explain the behavior of compounds from the actions of these elements. Here he distinguishes two processes: agglomeration and combination. The first is just a mixture of two components, which can usually be separated. The second brings about the existence of a new substance, which might have quite different properties from its constituents. His example: bronze is made from tin and copper.

He also investigates the nature of specific compounds, and gives an elementary classification of them – perhaps, the first in history. For example, substances that solidify in the cold and are dissoluble by fire are mostly water based. Those that are solidified by fire are mostly earth based.

Chemistry and physics are concerned with the matter out of which things are composed. However, they are not exclusively concerned with matter. Aristotle avoids reductionism in his theory of the formation of compounds. Things cannot be reduced to the matter out of which they are composed. In part, this is because Aristotle usually separates the matter/substance distinction from the part/whole distinction. 'What is a body composed of?' is not the same question as 'What parts does it have?' Earlier writers tended to confuse this distinction.

a) Matter The combination of the four elements explains the composition of compounds, such as tissue, milk, bark, stone. This explanation is a question of citing the material cause or the matter of things. We can see this in two ways. First, matter or stuff is not counted; we do not count milks or bloods. In Aristotle's terminology matter is not a (countable) substance. Second, matter is often uniform: a bit of blood is still blood.

b) Part/whole. Tissue or flesh is not a part of the human body; it is the matter. In contrast, parts, such as organs and hands, can be counted, and they depend on the whole. We cannot understand them without knowing their function with the whole. Furthermore they are not uniform: part of a hand is not a hand.

Here we have two very different kinds of explanation. To explain the parts of something, one needs to refer to their efficient and final causes. We explain the heart by showing what it does and how it works, and not by specifying what it is composed of. In other words, Aristotle realizes that understanding something does not always require taking it to bits. Referring to organic compounds, he writes:

> Such parts then, can come to be by heat and cold.. But the
> complex parts composed of these-for example, head, hand,
> foot - no one would believe to be composed in this way.
> Though cold and heat and motion are causes of bronze's and
> silver's coming to be, they are no longer the cause of a saw or
> a cup, or a box (Meteo 4.12)

Here we find a difference between chemistry and biology.

Animals

Aristotle's deep interest in animal life probably goes back to his
childhood. His father was the court physician to the father of Philip of
Macedonia. and Aristotle may well have learned some of his father's
medical skills. Many of the observations made by Aristotle date from
his time on the island of Lesbos, during the second period of his adult
life. Aristotle speaks with love of these studies:

> The craftsman of nature provides extraordinary pleasures for
> those who can recognize the causes in things and who are
> naturally inclined to philosophy.... We must not feel a
> childish disgust at the investigation of meaner animals. For
> there is something of the marvelous in all natural
> things....Similarly, we should approach the investigation of
> every kind of animal without being ashamed, since in each
> one of them there is something natural and something
> beautiful.

Approximately one fifth of his existing writings are dedicated to
biology. The *History of Animals* is a collection of data concerning the
similarities and differences between species, and might be viewed as a
prelude to classification. Aristotle collected information about as many
animal species as he could, around 500. He directly observed the
habits of bees, the copulation of cephalopods. the heart in the white of
the egg. He dissected about fifty kinds of animals. He also collected
information from fishermen, hunters and herdsmen.

According to Aristotle, though, science is about understanding causes, and not just gathering facts. To understand animals, he developed some of the major concepts we still use today in biological research. For example, he thinks systematically about the classification of animals. He debates the issues concerning inheritance and reproduction. He seeks to explain the functioning of physiological processes. In his scientific studies, Aristotle employs and puts to use his philosophical work on form and matter, the four causes and potential and actual.

Classification

For Aristotle, the world primarily consists of things which belong certain natural kinds, which define their essence. Classification is the definition of essence. The *History of Animals* is a collection of data concerning the similarities and differences between species, and as such might be viewed as a prelude to his account of classification. In the first book of *Parts of Animals*, Aristotle rejects Plato's attempt to classify by dichotomous division, through pairs of opposites, such as 'winged' and 'wingless.' According to Aristotle, such a classification has no structure, and violates the natural order, for example, by not placing all fish in one group.

How should animals be classified? In the work *Generation of Animals*, he rejects classification according to locomotion and argues for placing animals on a natural scale according to their state of development when they are born. This, he thinks, depends on the animal's body heat, which, he thinks, depends on blood. He, therefore, divides all animals into two groups; those with, and those without blood. His classification looks roughly like this:

With Blood	Without Blood
1. Humans	7. Cephalopods
2. Hairy quadrupeds	8. Crustacea
3. Sea mammals	9. Insects
4. Birds	10. Molluscs
5. Reptiles and amphibia	11. Zoophytes
6. Fish	

The first three types are capable having new born babies that are similar to the adult. In contrast, animals in the range from from birds to crustacea have eggs. Birds and reptiles have perfect eggs which do not grow after being laid. Fish, cephalopods, and crustacea have imperfect eggs, which need to develop even after being laid. Lower still come those animals that have grubs or larva, which Aristotle think of as a primitive pre-egg (Aristotle was not aware that grubs come from eggs). Lower still come those animals that reproduce asexually. The lowest kinds of animals generate spontaneously from the mud and earth.

When he mentions sponges and sea anemones, Aristotle claims that there is no strict boundary between animals and plants, and even between life and not life.

> Thus nature proceeds little by little from inanimate things to
> living creatures, in such a way that we are unable to
> determine the boundary line between them. (HA588b4)

Despite this, he seems to think of the differences between natural species as fixed.

Aristotle's classification is infused with the idea of higher and lower forms. The higher the more perfect. He conceived of the notions of end and purpose and natural development as fundamental to biology.

Physiological processes

With all organs and all physiological processes, Aristotle looks for the purpose, the objective served. For example, breathing cools the heart. Higher animals are naturally hotter and so they need to breathe a lot, and for this reason, they have lungs. Fish fulfil the same function by taking in water. So they have gills.

Aristotle also seeks mechanical explanations for these phenomena. For example, he compares the lungs to bellows, and he thinks that they are powered by the heat of the heart. The final cause gives the why, but not the how. The scientist needs both.

6
Metaphysics

Wisdom is more than knowledge. First, it is more than the sensory experience of particulars, for understanding requires that we must know how to group particular things according to universals or concepts or systems of classification. Following on from this, wisdom must involve knowing the most fundamental principles. To really understand as a wise person would, one must be able to give the most comprehensive explanation of things. Thirdly, such wisdom consists in understanding for its own sake. In this way it is different from technical knowledge gained for the sake of some practical purpose.

For Aristotle, the aim of metaphysics is to gain the type of knowledge which deserves to be called wisdom. It is the study of the most universal and primary of all causes. The title `metaphysics' does not come from Aristotle. The work we have of this name is a compilation of different shorter pieces written at different points in Aristotle's career. However, they all concern what we call metaphysics or what Aristotle might have called `first principles', or perhaps `philosophy' (love of wisdom).

As a compilation, the *Metaphysics* has 14 different books or chapters with different aims. To help you navigate, these are:

1) A -Alpha- introduces the idea of a science of first principles
2) α- little alpha- discusses the methodology of such a science
3) B- Beta-sets out 15 problems with arguments on both sides, that is for and against possible solutions

4) Γ- gamma- concerns metaphysics as the study of being qua being and tries to show how the principle of non contradiction is an assumption of meaning itself

5) Δ-Delta- is a lexicon explaining the different senses of about 40 philosophical terms

6) E – Epsilon- includes some brief remarks on truth

7) Z - Zeta -concerns substance and its relation to the form/matter distinction.

8) H - Eta- also concerns the form/matter distinction

9) Θ - Theta- concerns substance and its relation to actuality and potentiality

10) I- Iota- is about unity and plurality

11) K-Kappa- consists of a summary of previous points and parts of the physics.

12) λ - Lambda- concerns the notion of unchangeable substances and the unmoved mover

13) & 14) M and N- Mu and Nu- concern the existence of numbers and a criticism of Plato's ontology

These chapters or books have diverging aims and the overall book is more like a collection of essays than a single text. However, we can say that Aristotle's main aims are: first, to show how the study of the most fundamental principles is possible and what it consists in; and second, to answer the question 'what does reality consist in?' without making the mistakes committed by the pre-Socratics and Plato.

There are conflicts, and perhaps inconsistencies, between the different books of Aristotle's *Metaphysics*. For instance, some give different characterizations of what metaphysics is: the study of first principles, of being as such; of substance, and the study of the unmoved mover (or God).

Reality

Ultimately what is real? What does reality consist in? This is one of the central themes of the *Metaphysics*. Aristotle's answer to this question should be contrasted with the views of the pre-Socratic philosophers, on the one hand, and with those of Plato on the other.

The pre-Socratics are famous for their theories of what constitutes reality. Thales answered water. Anaximenes replied air. Anaximander, an indeterminate stuff, more primitive than any element. Aristotle rejects these answers wholesale. In effect, he argues that these theories attempt to describe the matter or the stuff of the universe, but that this does not tell us what reality consists in. According to Aristotle, reality consists in individual substances or particulars, such as individual plants, animals and persons. These substances are not identical with, nor reducible to, the matter out which they are composed. The pre-Socratic solution leaves out form.

On the other hand, Plato thought reality as consisted of eternal Ideas or Forms, transcending the realm of particulars in space and time. These Ideas are universals, such as beauty, justice, goodness. According to Aristotle, this reply to the question 'What is reality?' misunderstands form. It treats universals as if it were a substance.

Aristotle denies Plato's theory, but he admits the existence of Forms, Universals, and abstract objects, such as numbers. Aristotle's view is more subtle. He denies that universals or forms are substances. They exist, but Plato is mistaken about the type of existence they have.

Aristotle can find a middle path between the pre-Socratics and Plato, because he classifies types of existence. He recognizes that there are different ways in which things can exist. He makes this point by explaining the different ways in which something can be called 'healthy'. Sports, athletes, and diets are all said to be healthy, but they are so in different ways, notes Aristotle. He writes:

> Everything healthy is so-called with reference to health- some things by preserving it, some by producing it, some by being signs of health, some because they are receptive of it. (Γ2.1003a34)

These different ways of being healthy are connected. Diets, sports, complexions are healthy in a secondary or derivative way. The primary way of being healthy is to have a body in excellent functioning shape.

Aristotle uses this analysis of 'healthy' to better understand existence or 'to be.' The term 'exists' has a primary and also secondary uses, as does the term 'healthy'.

This classification of 'exists' or 'be' is the ontological reflection of Aristotle's categories. As we saw in chapter three, the categories are the basic types of predicates. They are the fundamental classification of word-types. Predicates are words which are said of subjects e.g. 'is white' is said of snow. Consequently, for Aristotle, predicates are subsidiary compared to subjects. This point is an important clue to Aristotle's ontology. This dependence of predicates on subjects in language reflects a parallel dependence in the world itself, because propositions are used to say true things of the world. Just as predicates depend on subjects, accidents or characteristics depend on individual particular substances. In other words, according to Aristotle, the categories of language are at the same time the categories of being.

In conclusion, Aristotle defines 'substance' as the primary existent. Ultimately reality consists in substances. The existence of other things is dependent on that of substance. The mistake of the pre-Socratics is to think of matter, or the stuff out which things are composed, as substance. Plato's mistake was to think of the universal Forms as substances. Both of these are dependent existences and hence not substance.

Furthermore, the notion of substance gives Aristotle a new approach to the question of what fundamentally exists. This question becomes equivalent to asking 'what is substance?' Before we look at Aristotle's answer to this question, we shall examine a slightly different approach to metaphysics.

Being as being

In book Gamma (4) of the *Metaphysics*, Aristotle defines a general science which studies being qua being, or being as being. This science is what we would call metaphysics, and in this part of the work, Aristotle is primarily concerned to show the nature of this study and show that it is possible.

What does the phrase 'being qua being' mean? It means that in metaphysics we investigate what exists, or the things which exist, with respect to their existence. The word 'qua' delineates under what aspect the thing in question is studied. For example, physiology studies the human being qua body, psychology the human being qua his or her behavior and mental states; sociology qua member of a society.

Having defined metaphysics in this way, Aristotle clarifies it further by answering puzzles which spring from the definition. Here is one. Effectively, the definition means that metaphysics investigates what it is to exist. Normally, sciences concentrate on what distinguishes their subject matter from other areas of investigation (for example, biology concerns the living rather than the dead). Usually specific sciences investigate a specific type of thing. However, metaphysics studies what existing things have in common. Aristotle says:

> These truths hold of everything that there is and not of some special kind of thing apart from others. (Γ3,1005a23)

Metaphysics is not concerned with specific types of things. Its subject matter is everything. Aristotle says: is that "it is not possible that either unity or existence should constitute a kinds of things." (B3 998b21) As a result of this, Aristotle initially doubts that metaphysics is possible. It has no subject matter. Metaphysics does not appear to be about anything, precisely because it is about everything. Existence is not a kind of thing.

Having raised this problem, Aristotle proceeds to answer it. In the final analysis, metaphysics is possible because there are different ways in which things can exist. A science does not require a single common notion; diets, exercise and medicines and pulse rates can all be studied within the medical sciences, even though they are healthy in different ways. This is because they are all related to the primary use of 'healthy'. So too for metaphysics and 'exists'. Aristotle concludes:

> It is clear then, that it is the task of a single science to study all the things that exist qua existent. (Γ2,1003b15)

Consequently, he claims that metaphysics is the study of concepts and principles which apply to existence qua existence, such as the three types of unity: sameness, similarity, and equality, and the three types of plurality: otherness, dissimilarity and inequality. It also investigates general principles or axioms, such as the principle of non-contradiction and the law of excluded middle, which apply to everything.

The Principle of Non-Contradiction

This principle states that it is impossible for the same attribute to belong and not belong to the same subject, in the same respect and at the same time. The snow cannot be both white and not white in the same way and at the same time.

The principle is equivalent to saying that a contradiction cannot be true. In *On Interpretation* (section 6) Aristotle defines a contradiction as a pair of opposed statements, one of which is an affirmation and the other of which is a denial.

Aristotle thinks that this principle is the firmest of all principles. It must be true because it is impossible to believe a contradiction. Here is Aristotle's demonstration of this: It is impossible for contraries to belong simultaneously to the same subject. A belief that contradicts another is the contrary of that belief. Thus it is impossible to believe both sides of a contradiction at the same time. For that would require the impossible – being in contrary states.

Aristotle is well aware that this argument presupposes the principle of non-contradiction. He claims that to show that the principle is the firmest of all, you have to employ the principle itself. Indeed he states the principle itself is impossible to demonstrate, precisely for this reason. Any formal demonstration of the principle would presuppose it. The demonstration would be circular. The principle is so basic it cannot be proved.

Nevertheless, Aristotle thinks that the principle can be supported with an informal argument. One could refute anyone who tries to deny the principle, by showing that by denying it, they assume it. If denying it involves its truth, then the principle is literally undeniable. Utter just one word: 'human.' If someone who says this means something by it, then 'being a human' must already exclude ' not being a human'. Consequently, a human cannot be a not human (in the same sense of the word). In short, the principle of non-contradiction is a necessary condition of the meaningfulness of any word.

What is substance?

What exists? What is real? What is being? For Aristotle, these questions can only be answered if we discover what substance is.

> The question which, both now and in the past, is continually posed and puzzled over is this: what is being? That is to say, what is substance? (Z1 1028b2)

The key to understanding reality and being is to know what substance is. This is because, as we have seen, for Aristotle, substance is primary. All other kinds of existing things depend on the existence of substance.

Aristotle answers the question in this way for the following reason. We could not answer the question what exists, by listing all particular things. The list could be infinite. We might try to list the types of things For example, we could list the types of mammals, the types of insects, and so on. However, clearly there is more general term which includes all these and more: it is 'animal.' If we listed all animals, then we would exclude plants, and there is a more general term which includes both: 'living things.' In this way, we can arrive at the highest and most general kinds of being. According to Aristotle, this ultimate list would be the categories. In other words, the categories indicate ways of being or existing. As we have already seen, among these categories, substance is primary. All other ways of existing depend on it.

The search for reality becomes the search for substance. However, the main job is not yet complete. Aristotle must show us what kinds of things are substances. To do that, he first tries to find general criteria something must satisfy to count as a substance and then, second, to discover what things satisfy those criteria.

To find these criteria, Aristotle defines 'substance' in Book Delta (5) of the *Metaphysics*:

> Things are called substances in two ways: a substance is whatever is an ultimate subject, which is no longer said of anything else, and a substance is a this so-and-so, which is also separable. ($\Delta 8$, 1071b23)

What is the first way? As we have already seen, according to Aristotle, all statements have a subject-predicate form. They consist in the assertion that a certain predicate is true of a subject: for example, the predicate 'is white' is true of the snow (the subject of the sentence). In the statement, 'white is a color' the subject is 'white', and the predicate is 'is a color'. In other words, 'white' can appear both as a predicate and as a subject. In this sense, is it is not an ultimate subject, and therefore, not a substance.

The second way: a 'this so-and-so' or a 'this something' is a strange phrase invented by Aristotle (a *tode ti*). What he means is that a substance is a particular – it is a this. It is also a so-and-so, because the individual thing has general characteristics which define what it is. Finally, he adds that substances must be separable. This probably means that their existence must be explainable without reference to the existence of other things. A smile is not a substance because it exists only because someone is smiling.

Later in the *Metaphysics*, Aristotle more or less discards the first way as an appropriate definition of substance. This leaves us with the second way: with the criterion that substance must be a primary and separate existent and that it must be a 'this so-and-so.'

In summary, we have seen why Aristotle thinks that metaphysics involves the study of substance. We have also examined Aristotle's definition of substance. Now we must discover what satisfies that definition. To complete the search, we need examples of substances.

In Search of Substance

In book Zeta of the *Metaphysics*, Aristotle completes his search for substance. He wants to show which items actually satisfy the criteria he has laid down. In chapter 3, he lists three general candidates for the title 'substance': substratum, essence, and universals. (He also mentions genus, but this is treated under universals).

Not Substratum

In book 3 Aristotle reconsiders his old definition of substance as a pure or ultimate subject. In the statement, 'the sphere is large', the subject is 'the sphere' and the predicate is 'is large'. A pure or ultimate subject would be something which is not a predicate of anything else. For example, 'the sphere' would not count as an ultimate subject because it can be a predicate of something else. For example in the statement 'That thing over there is a sphere', 'sphere' is no longer the subject, but rather is part of the predicate. According to Aristotle, the only thing which could satisfy this definition of an ultimate subject is bare matter, something which in itself has no characteristics but which supports all properties. This would be an X, an indeterminate substratum.

Aristotle argues that this substratum is not substance. This is because substratum is not a particular, a this, whereas, substance is.

Furthermore, substratum does not have independent existence. Pure substratum cannot exist independently of the things which are putatively made out of it, and therefore, it is not a substance.

Two clarifications. First, in arguing for this conclusion, Aristotle rejects the first part of the presumably earlier definition he gave of substance in the lexicon of *Metaphysics* Delta. Second, Aristotle rejects substratum as substance. Furthermore, probably, he also rejects the very idea of an indeterminate substratum, and does not identify it with matter.

Substance as Essence

In *Metaphysics* Z, sections 4-6, Aristotle turns to essence as a general candidate for the title 'substance.'

Essence is a what a thing is said to be in virtue of itself. It is its being per se. In the *Categories* and *On Interpretation*, in his study of predication, Aristotle distinguishes between essential and accidental predication.[1] Suppose the essence of being human is to be a rational animal. In which case, when we affirm that humans are rational animals, we are not just predicating a property of a subject. Instead, we are identifying what the subject really is, by specifying its essence. In an accidental predication, we attribute a non-essential property to a subject. For example, when we affirm that some human beings are musical, we are not specifying their essence, we are merely attributing a property to them. So, by specifying essence, we identify what the subject really is.

Aristotle argues that only substances really have essences; all other things have essence in a secondary way. Furthermore, to have an essence a thing must be strictly definable. According to Aristotle, the only thing which meets this criterion of being strictly definable are species. Therefore, he concludes that only species have essence and the only substances are species.

Clearly, Aristotle is working with a notion of real essence, as opposed to a merely verbal essence. The species human has a real essence which is to be a rational animal. Anything which is a human has to be a rational animal. In contrast to this, a tailor does not have to be a tailor. A tailor is only a person who happens to make clothes. He could change his occupation without ceasing to be. Being a tailor is not part of a person's essence. Aristotle concludes:

> In the primary and strict sense only substances have
> definition and essence, but other things have them also, only
> not in the primary sense. (Z.4 1029b13)

In other words, tailors, heroes and philosophers are not substances.
Human beings and other species are.

So far so good. There are two difficult and unresolved questions
about Aristotle's notion of essence. First, what is its relation to
universals? We will return to this question later. Second, what is its
relation to the individual? In chapter 6, Aristotle claims that things are
identical with their essence. This seems to indicate that individual
things in the natural world can have essences. For example, `Socrates
is human' makes an essential attribution to the individual, Socrates.
This is part of his essence. It identifies what he is.

Here is a radical difference between the philosophies of Plato and
Aristotle, which possibly dates back even to Aristotle's time in the
Plato's Academy. Plato denies that individual things have essences.
For him, essences belong to the separate world of Forms, and essential
predications can only be made of the Forms. In contrast, according to
Aristotle, essences are in the natural world, and consequently,
understanding must be directed towards this world and not to a
separate realm of Forms.

Substance as Form

In Chapters 7-9 of book Z, Aristotle relates the notion of
substance to that of form. Briefly, he claims that primary substance is
identical with definable form. He argues this on the grounds that the
form of a thing is what makes it what it is. This is what essence is, and
the earlier discussion of chapter 4 shows that the primary substances
are essences, which are species.

Not Universals

In chapter 13 of Z, Aristotle argues that universals should not be
considered as substances. He says:

But it seems impossible that any universal term should be a substance. For the substance of each thing is what is peculiar to it and does not belong to anything else; but a universal is common... (Z.13.1038b6)

Aristotle extends this argument against the claim that universals are substances into sections 14-16, where he also criticizes this aspect of Platonism. These arguments will be examined below. Having rejected universals as a candidate for substance, Aristotle can also reject genus, since the genus of a thing is a type of universal. (If human is the species, then the relevant genus is animal).

Interpretations

There are divergent interpretations of Aristotle's claim that primary substances are forms. In part, the difficulty is that Aristotle has made two major demands of the concept of substance. First, we have seen that substances are primary, because they have independent existence. Second, substances must be definable and knowable; hence their link to essence. These appear to be conflicting demands. The first makes us think that substances are individuals or particulars. The second might lean us towards thinking that substances are universals.

This difficulty has lead to very different interpretations of Aristotle, which we may broadly divide into three types, centered on how we should understand the crucial notion of form.

1) Form as Universal

According to the first view, the matter/ form distinction should be understood as follows: matter is identified by a stuff term, such a `bronze'. Form is identified by a property or universal term, such as `sphericality'. The resulting composite thing is a bronze sphere.

According to this interpretation, Aristotle's claim that primary substance is definable form should lead one to conclude that he thinks of substances as universals (such as sphericality). This idea makes good sense of the claim that substance must be definable. However, it makes less sense of Aristotle's claim that the existence of universals is dependent upon that of particulars, which is a fundamental difference between him and Plato. Consequently, the above interpretation of `primary substance is definable form' seems to contradict the claim that substance is an independent existent.

2) Form as neither particular nor universal

Some readers think that, in the book Z of the *Metaphysics*. Aristotle is trying to define a position which identifies form neither with universals nor particulars. According to this view, with his notion of substantial form, Aristotle is trying to forge a midway path between Platonic Forms on the one hand, and his own earlier view (in the *Categories*) of individuals as basic, on the other. According to this claim, the world does not fundamentally consist in individual people. animals and plants, but rather in the species themselves. or in natural kinds. The world is really divided into these kinds. and these are basic.

3) Form as the particular

According to the third interpretation, the form is the individual thing itself.[2] For example, the form of a house is a dwelling. According to this interpretation, the matter/form distinction is the distinction between the constituent and the thing constituted. The matter is the constituent (i.e. the bronze). The form is the thing constituted (i.e. the sphere). The form is a particular thing, the sphere and not the universal, sphericality. For a form to exist is for matter to be differentiated in a certain way.

This third interpretation would fit well with the idea that. according Aristotle. essences also are particular things. It should be pointed out again that if Aristotle does think that individual things have essences, then it might be more accurate to claim that these things are their essence, rather than that they have their essence. This because essence is what a thing is per se. In this case. when Aristotle speaks of essences. he is referring to individual things. If this is right. then Aristotle's dual characterization of substance as essence and of substance as form would both imply that substances are particular things.

These three broad categories do not exhaust the possible interpretations of Aristotle's notion of form, nor of the text itself. For example, one possibility is that Aristotle flirts with a position similar to 3) above in chapters 7-9 of the Metaphysics Z, but ends up with a view as outlined in 2) in chapter 17 of Zeta. Possibly and tentatively. the general view which makes the best overall sense of the text is that primary substances are individuals or particulars, but only insofar as they are members of natural kinds. Returning to the original definition in book Delta, substances must be a 'this so-and-so.' The 'this' indicates that they be individuals, and the 'so-and –so' specifies that they be natural kinds or species. In other words. we identify a particular individual as a primary substance if and only if we refer to it as a natural kind or species.

Summary

In conclusion, Aristotle restricts what may count as substance to what we might call natural objects, as individuals belonging to natural kinds.

1) He excludes matter or stuff, such as gold and blood. These are not individual things. They are what some individual things are made of. Hence they are dependent existents and are not substances.

2) On the same grounds, he also excludes substratum.

3) He excludes Universals on the grounds that they are dependent existents (Z.13)

4) He excludes things which by their nature are only parts, and hence are dependent existents. For example, a hand is essentially a body part; what it is should be defined in relation to the whole body. Hence it is not a substance

5) He excludes collections of other things; for example, a flock of geese is not a substance. Its existence depends on that of the individual geese.

6) He also excludes particular things described in non-essential ways. For example, a soldier is not a substance. The essence of the individual, who happens to be a soldier, is to be human. Therefore, it is humans who are substances and not soldiers. (Z.4)

7) He excludes artifacts from the list of substances on the grounds that their nature is entirely dependent on that of the wood or material from which they were made.

Plato and the Forms

Now we can see how different Aristotle's ontology is from Plato's. Plato argued for the independent existence of universals or

Forms. He argued that, in addition to beautiful particular things, there exists the abstract entity beauty. Similarly for all other predicates.

One of Plato's main arguments for the theory of Forms is that only in this way can we explain science and knowledge generally. Science requires knowledge of the Forms. According to Plato, the alternative would be to admit that systems of classification are arbitrary or subjective, as the Sophists had argued. Protagoras had claimed that man is measure of all things, and that, since humans vary from culture to culture, there can be no objective measures. One of the main underlying motivations of Plato's theory of Forms is to avoid that kind of subjectivism.

Aristotle wants to deny Plato's theory, but he does not want to embrace subjectivism or Sophism. He thinks that both are mistaken. His theory of the categories permits him to argue against Plato without embracing the other extreme. This is because Aristotle does not deny that forms or universals exist. Instead, he denies that they have independent existence. Aristotle thinks that universals exist, but that their existence is derivative or parasitic. For him, beauty exists only insofar as particular beautiful things do. In other words, according to Aristotle, for accidents or universals to exist, it is necessary and sufficient for individual substances to exist.

In books Mu and Nu of the *Metaphysics*, Aristotle defends this approach with regard to mathematics. Aristotle tries to refute the Platonic claim that numbers are things distinct from the everyday objects that we can count. Similarly, according to Aristotle, geometrical figures are not things distinct from the surfaces, lengths and volumes of the physical bodies we see. In this way, Aristotle hopes to show how mathematics is compatible with his naturalistic ontology, and to undermine what might seem to be an important support for the Platonic notion of the Forms.

He also avoids two problems inherent in Plato's theory. First, if numbers are Forms, or substances separate from the world of concrete objects, then how do we know them? For Plato knowledge of the Forms must be gained by reason. In contrast, as we have seen, Aristotle stresses the importance of sense-perception and induction in knowledge. Plato and Aristotle have very different theories about the nature of reality, and this has important implications for their views of science, learning and knowledge

The second problem: if mathematical objects exist as Forms in a separate realm, how can we use them to describe everyday things? More generally, one of Aristotle's main arguments against the Forms as separate substances is that they have no explanatory power.

According to Aristotle, there are no ideal triangles and circles. The mathematician studies ordinary physical circles and triangles. He or she does not study them qua or as physical things. He or she studies them as something idealized and abstracted from the conditions of physical change. An ideal circle is nothing distinct from a real circle idealized. Mathematics and physics deal with the same substances, but qua different aspects.

Theology

The last part of the Metaphysics seems to argue for a view of the science entirely different from the rest of the treatise. It defines a science of theology, a study of God.

The *Physics* argues that there must be an unmoved mover. Aristotle takes up the same argument in the *Metaphysics*, to conclude that this must be an eternal and unchanging substance. Aristotle's argument for this conclusion has two premises. The first premise: if all substances were destructible, everything would be destructible, because substances are primary existents. The second premise: time and movement cannot come into being nor cease to be. Consequently, there is something indestructible. Therefore, there must be an indestructible substance.

Furthermore, he argues that this eternal substance must be 'an eternal principle whose essence is actuality.' The essence of this substance is actuality. It consists of pure activity, without any power or potentiality. This must be so, says Aristotle, because "that which is potentially may possibly not be." Met $\lambda.6.1071b4$. In other words, to explain motion, it is not enough to cite the existence of something which is potentially an unmoved mover (since the existence of such a thing is compatible with there being no movement at all).

What does it mean to say that the essence of the unmoved mover is pure actuality? To be completely actual, the eternal substance must be without any potential; it must be pure activity. The activity in question could not be physical, because all material things are changeable, and the unmoved mover must be an eternal substance. Therefore, its actuality must consist in a purely spiritual activity. According to Aristotle, the only possible unchanging, spiritual activity is pure thought or contemplation.

Trying to establish more about this eternal substance. Aristotle claims that the unmoved mover

> Exists of necessity; qua necessary its being is good and it is in this way (as good i.e. as object of love and desire) that it is a principle. (Met λ.7 1072a26)

Aristotle's idea is that all physical movement implies a contact of mover and moved and hence a movement of the mover. In other words, the unmoved mover cannot cause motion in the normal way. The only alternative is that it cause motion by being the object of desire and love.

Aristotle thought that God directly causes the daily rotation of the outermost stars around the still Earth by inspiring in them love and desire. The outer stars desire to live an unchanging, eternal life, and in an effort to emulate this, they perform the next best thing-continuous, unbroken movement, in a circle. This outermost rotation causes movement in the other spheres, which causes the planets, sun and moon to rotate too, and which causes the motions in the sublunary world, which we described in Chapter five. In this way, all change comes from the eternal substance. There is an unmoved mover, even though there is no first event, no creation. Matter has always existed.

The important point is that the unmoved mover must cause change by being loved. This establishes the nature of the eternal substance. It must be something essentially good.

Aristotle begins to call the eternal substance `God'. Because He is essentially good, God's eternal thoughts must be directed towards what is best. What is best is Himself. Aristotle does not mean that God thinks about Himself thinking about Himself...Possibly, the idea is that, with God, there is no difference between the object of thought and the thought itself. God thinking cannot be distinguished from the existence of things He thinks. As we shall see, divine contemplation is an important notion for Aristotle's ethics, because it has implications for his view of human nature.

---

[1] In the *Categories* and *On Interpretation*. However, these are not the words he uses.

[2] D. Wiggins 1980 and W.Charlton, 1970

7
Psychology

In the 17th century physics portrayed matter as an inert substance obeying mechanical causal laws in determinate patterns. The idea of ourselves as self-conscious beings who freely choose our actions does not fit well into this picture of matter. Hence the mind-body problem: how can a conscious being consist of inert matter?

Although Aristotle is concerned with the mind-body relation, it is not quite within the context of our contemporary problem. For, first, despite his views on scientific explanation, Aristotle does not have the modern view of matter. Secondly, with some important qualifications, Aristotle views humans as animals with some distinctive biological functions, such as the capacity to laugh, speak and think. As a consequence of these two points, he is less concerned with the mental-physical distinction, and is more concerned with the difference between the living and the dead. Also, as a result, for him, any theory of the human being must include nutrition, respiration and digestion, as well perception, memory and desire.

For these reasons it is difficult to translate the Greek word 'psuche.' It is sometimes translated as 'soul', but this English word is permeated with the Christian idea of a non-material thing. The word 'mind' has similar connotations, and it is usually contrasted with the modern conception of matter. As we shall see, for Aristotle, plants have a *psuche*, because they are living, animate beings. He does not mean that they have minds. Perhaps the best solution is to anglify the Greek word 'psuche' as psyche.

The Soul as Form

In Book II of *On the Soul*, Aristotle introduces his own theory by claiming that every living body is both a form and matter. The psyche is the form of the person. Flesh and bone is the matter out which we are composed. According to Aristotle, to understand the relation between the mind and body, we must grasp the relation between form and matter.

For example, take a bronze sphere. The object itself is a substance, which is both form and matter. Form is the thing constituted and the matter is the constituent. The form identifies what the object essentially is. Therefore, the form is the sphere itself. The matter is the stuff out of which it is composed (i.e. the bronze).

The view needs to be stated very carefully. Notice that in the above explanation, I did not claim that the bronze sphere is two composed of two elements, form and matter. Expressed in this way, it sounds as if the form and matter could exist on their own, independently of the sphere. Aristotle wants to deny that form and matter are independent things. Therefore, it is best not to call them elements. Notice also that I did not affirm that the bronze sphere has a form. It is more accurate to say the sphere itself is the form, since the form is not a universal. Aristotle's view is that there is only thing. Described qua matter, it is bronze; described qua form, is it a sphere.

Given this, there are two mistakes to avoid: first, to think of the form as an additional non-material thing, in the way that Plato does, and second, to try to reduce the sphere to its matter (i.e. the bronze) in the way that some of the pre-Socratics would.

Mind and Body

This simple example illustrates the relation between substance, form and matter. It helps us to understand Aristotle's view of the psyche since it is the form of the body.

In the case of the soul, the form is more complex, but basically, the relations between substance, form and matter remain the same. The important point is the following: there is only one thing, namely the individual person. Described as form, this person is psyche or soul identified by its essential functions. Described as matter, this person is flesh and bone. Neither the form nor the matter should be thought of as separate substances.

This insight is still illuminating today. It cuts across simplistic versions of the debate between the dualist and reductive materialist. A dualist regards the soul as a non-material thing. Aristotle would insist that this kind of dualism involves treating the form of a person as though it were a separate substance. Reductive materialism, on the other hand, treats the person as though they were nothing more than the matter out they are composed and ignores form.

In contemporary terms, we can put Aristotle's theory as follows. A person can be described in two radically different ways: physically and psychologically. The psychological descriptions are given in terms of what the person wants, believes, hopes, feels and does. Such descriptions do not indicate the existence of a separate entity, the mind. They apply to the person, but the psychological descriptions cannot be reduced to descriptions of the person's physical state.

Given these clarifications, the important question now is: 'what is the form of a human being?' since this is equivalent to asking 'what is the soul or psyche of a human?' First, some more details regarding Aristotle's conception of form. He has three related ways to explain form

1) In terms of essence

According to Aristotle, any particular thing or individual substance can be characterized as a form which is its essence. By essence, he means the characteristics that a thing must have to be what it is. Since things are always definable in terms of their essence, and only things with an essence can be defined, essence itself cannot be defined. The psyche is an essence; it does not have one.

2) In terms of actuality

Aristotle also defines the psyche in terms of actuality. After characterizing the psyche as "the form of a natural body which potentially has life" (412a20), he also describes it as "the first actuality of a natural body which potentially has life." (412a27). Aristotle says that form stands to matter as actual stands to potential. An undifferentiated piece of bronze (i.e. matter) is only potentially a statue. When it has the form of a statue, then it actually is a statue. In other words, matter is merely potential; form is actual

When applied to the more complex case of the human psyche, there are two levels of the potential/actual distinction. First, a being can have the required capacities, but not be exercising them. For example, consider a scientist who is asleep. Is she actually intelligent? Yes, because she has certain capacities, even though she is not using them now. This actuality at the first level. Second, the person can be actually exercising the capacities in question. Aristotle says that the soul or psyche is actual in the first of these two ways, rather than the second. Thus, he says:

> Waking is actuality which corresponds to cutting and seeing, the psyche is actuality corresponding to sight, that is the capacity of the organ. (412b2)

The soul is the first kind of actuality, and to achieve that, a body must have the appropriate organs. According to Aristotle, every capacity requires an organ (except possibly the vexed case of nous or active reason which we will discuss later). Therefore, Aristotle's account of the soul requires a description of the functioning of the organs.

3) In terms of function

To explain the idea of form, Aristotle compares a natural body to a tool, and then to the eye.

> Suppose that a tool, c.g. an axe, were a natural body, then being an axe would be its essence and so its psyche; if this disappeared from it, it would have ceased to be an axe...Suppose that an eye were an animal –sight would have been its psyche... (412b11-22)

Sometimes Aristotle explains form in terms of natural function, and this is closely linked to the reference to organs, because organs perform various functions.

Levels

All living things must have a capacity to feed. In addition, animals have the capacity to perceive and humans, the capacity to reason. These are the essential functions of the different kinds of living things. By explaining soul in terms of these functions, Aristotle can give an account of different levels of psyche. He thinks that this layered approach is appropriate than a general theory. He says:

It is now evident that a single account can be given of *psuche* only in the same way as it is for figure. For, as in that case, there is no figure apart from triangle.... so here there is no *psuche* apart from those just mentioned (II. 3.414b20)

Plants and animals

Plants are the simplest form of life. They have the powers of nutrition: to eat, grow, decay and reproduce. These functions define the nutritive soul. He says:

Since nothing except what is alive can be fed, what is fed is the animate body and just because it is animate. Hence food is essentially related to what has *psuche* (II.4.,416b9)

Eating food is not just a question of gaining mass. Food must be something which nourishes, and hence it is linked to growth.

Animals have the same nutritive capacities as plants. However, in addition, they have the power of sense-perception. Because of this, they have imagination, which is a decayed form of perception. And because of this, they have desire, which is stimulated by perception and imagination. Finally, because of desire, they have the capacity to do things, to move.

According to Aristotle, these animal functions (perception, desire and action) are conceptually linked. The last could not exist without the first. Perception provides desire with its objects. And desire could not exist without pursuit.

It follows that no body which has a soul is able to move but unable to perceive. (III.12, 434a37)

Furthermore, perception would have no point without desire, and desire would have no point without the power to pursue.

The basis of the animal psyche is perception, the simplest form of which is touch. What is perception? As we might expect, Aristotle treats perception sense by sense. In each case, however. Aristotle describes a physical and physiological process, which is the material aspect of perception. Referring to Plato. Aristotle says that to describe the functions of the psyche without giving any specification of the bodily conditions is an absurdity (I.3. 407b12). This is because what a thing is made of places physical constraints on what it can do. To do its job, an axe must be hard. Similarly. mental functions require the physically appropriate organs. The distinctive capacity of the sense organs is to receive

perceptible forms without matter, as wax receives the ring's seal engraving without its iron or gold. (II.12, 424a18)

Basically, this means that the organs have the capacity to become similar to the thing affecting them. This similarity is then transmitted to a center. which Aristotle thought was the heart, and which is in fact, of course, the brain. J.L. Ackrill suggests that we should think of this process as the putting of information in a code. For Aristotle. the whole sensory system of an animal is really one. All sense organs converge on the single primary organ, because it is the animal or person himself who touches, sees, hears etc.

In the case of seeing, the eyes must be able to transmit color, which is relevant kind of perceptible property. The eyes can transmit this because they are made of transparent water. In conclusion, by definition. the eyes must be capable of seeing, and to see, they must have a transparent element. Consequently, the material make-up of the eye is an essential part of a theory of vision.

According to Aristotle, a proper explanation of any mental function will identify the object of the relevant condition. The object of sight is the visible. When we describe the object of sight as such, we identify it as a color. However, this does not mean that we can only see colors, because the object of sight can be described incidentally, as a person or as some object. In this way, it can be said that we see ordinary objects. A proper account of a mental function will be also an embodied account. For example, the philosopher might define anger as the desire to return pain. The physician might define it as the boiling of blood around the heart. An embodied account of anger would involve both the material and formal description of the state. (I,1,403b1)

Reason

Reason. the capacity to understand. is the distinctive function of human beings. Aristotle says that a person never thinks without some imagery. Thought depends on imagination. which in turn depends on perception.

In Book III. chapter 5 of *On the Soul*, Aristotle distinguishes passive from active intellect. Passive intellect works by becoming all things. It acquires the form. In this sense. reasoning is like perception. in which we receive a perceptual form or likeness of the object perceived, except that for reason. the form is intelligible. It is the essence or definition of the thing. Passive reason, a perceiver of definitions. contemplates essences. On the other hand, active reason works by making all things. Aristotle compares it to light. which makes potential colors actual. As such. he suggests that active reason is necessary for passive reason.

As we have seen. Aristotle treats mental faculties as inseparable from their physical basis. The two are only separable in account because they are form and matter. However. Aristotle claims that active reason is immortal. eternal. divine and does not depend on matter for its functioning. It is pure form without matter. It can exist without the person.

Remember that Aristotle affirms that matter and form are inseparable, except in account. This claim follows logically from the very nature of the form-matter distinction, as explained in the previous chapter. It seems that Aristotle's views on active reason are incompatible with the very basis of his metaphysics. The account of active intellect requires the idea of form without matter. However. this implies that forms are universals with an independent existence. rather than being merely an abstracted aspect of individual things. This account apparently requires treating universals as a substance. This part of Aristotle's ontology is similar to Plato's and some writers have suggested that Aristotle's account of active intellect belongs to an earlier period during which he was more under the influence of Plato.

Aristotle's biological view of the mind conflicts with his view that active reason is something divine and immortal. Much the same might be said about *Metaphysics* λ (Lambda), where Aristotle explains his views concerning the unmoved mover. His naturalistic view of substance in the rest of the *Metaphysics* apparently conflicts with his theology. Nevertheless. the theology and the notion of active reason have a role in his ethics.

8
Ethics

Two Questions

Everyone has thought about the questions that Aristotle discussed in the book, *Nichomachean Ethics*. Usually, we quickly dismiss these questions because they turn out to be so devilishly difficult. There are really just two questions: 'what is the best way to live?' and 'how do we determine what is the right thing to do when it is not obvious?'

Concerning the first question, we all realize that we have only a limited number of years on this earth and this may be all that we have. We want to spend the years wisely, but exactly how should we do that? What should we devote ourselves to?

Part of the issue of living a good life for most people is doing the right thing. Often it is not difficult to know what that is and shoot. We know that when someone in a car asks us directions to the nearest hospital because they have an emergency with a sick child, we should not intentionally give them incorrect directions. We are not puzzled about what is right in these kinds of cases, but often matters are not so simple. Sometimes as sincerely as we would like to do the right thing, we do not know what it is.

While the *Ethics* focuses on how an individual should best live their life, and how individuals should decide what is right, Aristotle thought that these questions leave out a very important factor. It is true that we all have our own lives to live and our own decisions to make. but we do not live or decide in a vacuum. We are social creatures. part of a community. A complete answer to these questions would have to include a consideration of what the best society is to live in, and how a society should make decisions. But one cannot answer all questions at the same time. and so to simplify matters. these questions will be put aside until the next chapter. Let us just concentrate on the individual case, always remembering that this is only part of the story

Reason

The first step in answering the two fundamental questions is an obvious one. although it is not trivial. To understand what is the best life. we have to have some way to consider life. What exactly is our life? Is it a collection of experiences? Should we consider it as a series of events? Or is it something else?

Aristotle's answer is that a life is actually something else--a series of actions. We do not just passively live. but we actively act. That is the first key concept that will enable us to see what is the best life. Living is something that we do. and that means that we have a certain amount of control over our own lives. We will be able to see what the best life will be if we first put our own life into the category of action.

The Goal of Action--Happiness--Eudaimonea

If our life is an action, then what is its goal? Every action that we intentionally perform is aimed at some goal, for we do things to accomplish an end. Again, this is obvious, but not trivial. Consider someone digging a hole in the middle of a city park. We ask him, why are you doing that? What are you trying to accomplish? He responds that there is no goal for what he is doing. What could he mean? Is he some kind of performance artist or a vandal? Is this aerobic exercise? The moral is that we cannot make sense of any action in which the person doing it sincerely claims not to have some aim in mind.

This leads to the next point. The actions that we perform have goals. and these goals can often be questioned themselves as to why the individual performing them wants to achieve them. For example. consider our friend digging the hole in the park again and imagine that he actually does have a goal in mind. He is digging the hole because he is planting a tree for the Park Department. Digging the hole is part of his job. But working at a job is an action also, and we can ask him what he is trying to accomplish by doing that. He answers that he works to get a salary. What is the point of that? We can go on and on this way, and probably we will reach a point where our friend gets tired of these questions and thinks that there is nothing more to say. Eventually, he will provide some answer that is ultimate, and that is the point at which the questions should stop. But what is this ultimate stopping point?

According to Aristotle the ultimate answer is happiness. All of our actions ultimately aim at happiness, and when that answer is given, there is nothing more to ask about. It makes no sense to ask so: 'What are you trying to accomplish, by aiming at happiness?' Happiness is the one thing we want just for itself. and not to accomplish any other end, for it is complete in itself. It stops the line of questions, and it is the goal of the actions that constitute our lives.

The English word 'happiness' is the usual translation of the Greek word 'eudaimonea' that Aristotle used as the name of the goal of all of our actions. As is the case with many translations. the term 'happiness' does not quite mean the same thing as 'eudaimonea'. To us English speakers, 'happiness' has the connotation of being content, of sitting back and enjoying a beautiful sunset, or else finding out that one has just won the lottery. This is not what Aristotle had in mind. Eudaimonea is the state that is the goal of all of our actions, but he had a more active conception in mind. The state of eudaimonea occurs when someone is using all of their powers to their fullest extent. and things are going as well as they could. Many scholars have thought that 'flourishing' provides a better account of what Aristotle was getting at by using the term 'eudaimonea' than does 'happiness', and that is the view that will be adopted from here on. Aristotle's claim that the goal of our actions is happiness means that our actions are aimed at our flourishing as human beings. being healthy, active, fulfilling our potential, and living as well as we can. Aristotle says that this point about eudaimonea is a truism. It is good to keep it in mind. but the real question is, how does one achieve eudaimonea. That is not so obvious.

Functions

At this point in the *Ethics*, Aristotle begins to talk about functions, and in particular the function of human beings. This part of Aristotle is difficult to understand, because to us, the idea that human beings have a particular function sounds obscure. It is true enough that each part of the body has a function. The function of the eye is to see, of the ear to hear, etc. Furthermore, different individual human beings have functions, such as a doctor to heal. From this Aristotle concludes that human beings in general have a function, and knowing what it is will be the key to living a flourishing life.

This seems to be a very questionable inference on Aristotle's part, one that seems to be committing the fallacy of composition. This mistake in reasoning occurs when one concludes that a quality that can be found in every part of a whole must also be a quality of the whole too. For example, it would be bad reasoning to conclude that a range of mountains is a large range, because each individual mountain is huge.

So there are two problems with Aristotle's view of the function of human beings. First, it is not clear what he means by that concept in the first place, and the second is that the reasons he gives for why humans do have a function seem fallacious. We could at this point conclude that Aristotle was just muddled, or we could spend a great deal of time trying to entangle him from these various traps. But instead of doing that, it will be more helpful to provide an explanation of Aristotle's view based on some points of biology that Aristotle would have used himself, or that he would have used if had the information we have about the subject of biology.

Biology, Structure, Activity and Rankings

As was shown above, Aristotle had a great interest in understanding plants and animals and then figuring out what was necessary for them to live well and flourish. This interest in biology was very crucial for our understanding *eudaimonea*, because Aristotle thought that we are biological creatures--we are animals, and that it is useful for us to think about ourselves in this way.

When we examine animals, we see that they come in a wide variety of structures, and that they live very different kinds of lives.

There is a close connection between the structure and the type of life. Birds are small animals with very light bones, and this is clearly related to the fact that they spend a great deal of their lives flying around.

When we compare animals with each other, in terms of their structure and activities, we can make rankings on various dimensions that reveal which animals rank highly on which dimensions. For example, consider the bodies of seals: it is striking that they are so stream-lined. They have sleek, smooth bodies. In fact, most animals like goats, frogs and monkeys would rank far below seals on a ranking of the dimension of "streamlinedness". This characteristic of seals is clearly related to the fact that they are such excellent swimmers. A seal on a land is a clumsy thing to see, but the worst seal swimmer is undoubtedly far better than the best Olympic champion. The physical structure of the seal provides the explanation for their excellence as swimmers. They, unlike us, are built according to the hydrodynamic principles that make for speedy and graceful swimming.

Let us apply this Aristotelian analysis to monkeys. Compared to other animals, they have very small bodies and unusually long limbs with hands and feet that can grasp, and often a long prehensile. They also have eye-hand-foot coordination that is far above that of four limbed animals. These physical characteristics explain why monkeys are such gifted acrobats. Again, the clumsiest monkey will outdo the best human circus performer. Humans are too large, our limbs are too short, and our coordination and reflexes are too slow to be able to swing through trees and vines with the ease and grace of monkeys.

The point of this kind of analysis for Aristotle is that it reveals what sort of life a particular kind of animal is built for, or in what kind of situation the particular animal will flourish and find its own *eudaimonea*. Given their build, and what they are good at, seals will thrive when they live in an aquatic environment. But put a seal in a tree in a jungle, and nothing but disaster will happen to it. But a monkey is built just for being in that tree in the jungle. It has all that it needs to live a fine life there. But put a monkey in the ocean, and it will not live very long. The general pattern then is that structural qualities indicate what activities an animal will excel at, and that indicates what sort of life would be best for that particular animal.

Structure, Activities, and Rankings of Human Beings

When we look at the biological structure of human beings and compare them to other animals, the question to ask is, 'What are the distinctive structural qualities of human beings?' On what dimension would humans be ranked first? It certainly would not be in general size or the powerful nature of our muscles. We are not the best, or even that close to the top in those particular structural qualities. Our striking feature is the size and complexity of our brains. It is true that elephants and whales have even bigger brains than ours, but they also have bigger bodies. When one considers their size, their brains are not so impressive. Also, some little animals like mice and squirrels might have a similar brain to body size as we have; nevertheless, their brains are still tiny, and lack the complexities of the human brain.

The next question is 'What activity is connected to this structural feature?' The answer is clear; humans rank number one in the feature of reasoning and thinking. Humans can perform mental feats that are beyond the most intelligent of any other animal species. Because of our huge brains, no other animal can predict the future as well, can learn, can communicate, or can plan as well as we do.

A point of clarification regarding the role of brain in human thinking. Aristotle did not know that it is the brain that enables us to perform these activities. While Aristotle had mistaken ideas about the biological bases of thought and reason, our more up-to-date knowledge would fit in very smoothly with his basic approach. The distinctive structural characteristics of an animal will indicate what that animal excels at, and we now know that our very special brains enable us to perform certain activities at a level much beyond that of other animals.

Following the Aristotelian pattern of analysis, this all points to the kind of life we are built to live and in the kind of situation in which we are likely to flourish. Human beings are built to live in a situation where they can use their large brains to figure things out, to plan, and to communicate complex messages. Aristotle grouped all of these various activities under the rubric of reasoning. Humans excel at reasoning and that means that we will thrive in situations where we can use these capacities. On the other hand, if humans find themselves in situations where they cannot reason, they will not do well. They will be like seals in trees, and monkeys in a swimming pool.

Reasoning as the Human Function

The Aristotelian analysis of structure, activities and rankings provides an explanation of what he meant by function. An animal's function is expressed by the activities it excels at, and the excellence of an animal's activities are matters that can be determined by examination structures and related activities of the animal. Reason is our function in this Aristotelian sense, and that means that reasoning will be a very important feature of a thriving human life. Reasoning is not sufficient in itself to make a good life, just as being in an aquatic environment is not enough to make a happy seal. For the seal to be happy, it also needs food, the presence of other seals, etc. For a human to be happy, it also needs more than the opportunity to reason. But reasoning will certainly be one important factor in a good life.

When Aristotle said that reasoning is important for humans, he did not necessarily mean that humans will only be happy if they devote themselves to intellectual pursuits like studying philosophy or doing logic problems. He had a broader notion of what reasoning meant. He thought that a full human life would require some use of the outstanding human intellectual capacity, but the object of the capacity could be any number of things. Craftsmen thinking how to make shoes, and plumbers determining how to unplug toilets are both using reason in Aristotle's sense.

The kind of life that Aristotle thought was devoid of reasoning was that of a slave, condemned to perform a repetitive task without the chance to choose or develop a skill. Even if other aspects of life were well provided for, it is difficult to think that a human being would be happy in that kind of situation. Slavery was a common feature in Aristotle's society, and he undoubtedly noticed that these people did not appear to be very happy.

Since slavery no longer exists in our society, we have to think of other examples of people who do not use reasoning in their lives. Probably the closest example to what he had in mind would be the workers on assembly lines, who even if well paid, just sit there and tighten bolts for eight hours a day. This has to be an excruciating life for human beings, for we have these big brains that need to be engaged by something. Aristotle would predict that people who have to do this kind of work are not going to be very fulfilled.

Another prediction that Aristotle might make is that people who spend long hours just watching mindless television shows will also not be that happy. One might be well-fed, well-clothed, and in pleasant temperature, but even so, just staring at stupid programs is not enough to activate our advanced mental powers. This is not the kind of life that would provide *eudaimonea* for human beings.

These predictions and applications of Aristotle's views show that there is an empirical element to his view. He was not the kind of philosopher who just thought about how things must be and if the world did not agree would say so much the worse for the world. Aristotle was an empirically minded thinker. If his predictions are incorrect about what kinds of lives are fulfilling to people, then his view collapses. His theory is based on observation.

External Goods

Aristotle was different than most philosophers in not being a monomaniac. He did not think just one thing was necessary for a good life, and as long as that one thing was present, everything would be fine. In this he was quite different than his teacher Plato, as well as most other philosophers, who get one idea and then think they have found the secret for everything.

In particular, Aristotle realized that reasoning, while important for a good human life is clearly not the whole story. One could be in a situation in which one has ample opportunities to use one's big brain, and still be miserable because of other factors, such as having a disease, or noisy neighbors, or being hit by a bus. In any human life there will always be a number of factors over which a person has no control, and yet, these factors contribute greatly to how well one's life will go.

Aristotle called these factors "external goods" and he provided a list of the major ones. Again, it is important to realize that Aristotle lived in a society that was technologically primitive in comparison to ours, and so he had no idea that some aspects of life could be controlled. Nevertheless, we face the same difficulty, which is that a good portion of our life prospects is determined by luck.

For example, Aristotle thought that good looks were one of these external factors. His Greek culture was maybe even more obsessed by physical beauty than is ours, and so he thought that being ugly would detract from a good life. We now have the capability of plastic surgery to fix things up. but even so, some people are still grotesque. If one is unfortunate in this way, it doesn't necessarily condemn one to misery, but it certainly makes achieving happiness a great deal more difficult.

Another external good is wealth. For Aristotle. one's financial prospects were determined almost 100% by the luck of birth. People with rich parents would be rich, and those with poor parents would be poor. We believe that we have a great deal of mobility, but as a matter of fact. for us too, the vast majority of people will wind up being in the same economic class as their parents. There is only somewhat more movement than there was in Aristotle's society. Aristotle did not think that wealth was absolutely essential for a good life. but it helps. It is hard to live well. have *eudaimonea*, when one is desperately poor

Aristotle lists a number of other external goods: health, reputation, and good children (not just children). He does not have much more to say about them because he thought they were matters of chance and luck. and so there really is not that much to be said. Either one is lucky or one is not. There is not much one can do about external goods. Nevertheless, they do contribute to a good life, not in the sense that they are necessary or sufficient. but rather that they help.

A good life is like a good cake in that there are a number of ingredients that contribute to the final product. It is possible to have a tasty cake without sugar. but sugar certainly is an ingredient that makes it more likely that the cake will turn out well. The same is true for external goods. If one has a good share of them, and also one is able to exercise one's reason. then one is the best position to have what Aristotle called a "blessed life." But even if one did not do so well in terms of external goods, all is not hopeless. But being realistic, it will be much more difficult to achieve *eudaimonea*.

Virtue

For Aristotle the best life will be one in which one has good luck with the external factors and one is also using the distinctive human capacity of reason. But there is more to be said about reason . For here we are with our huge brains. that are outstanding in figuring out puzzles and problems. Let us apply it to the problem of living the best life, and see if it can provide us with any useful information on this topic.

On what should we focus our powerful reasoning abilities? What would provide us with the most useful information for improving our lives? Would it be worthwhile to for us to figure out how to make a fortune on the stock market? Being rich would help, but this may really only be a matter of luck. Should we try to obtain religious knowledge? Would it help us to know if God exists and how to get eternal life? This might help us in the afterlife, but it is not clear it would improve our current life. Also, as powerful as our brains are, they may not find satisfactory answers to the religious questions.

Perhaps the most useful question is, what features of life, of those we can control, contribute the most to living a good life? Aristotle's answer is again an empirical one, based on his observations and what other people have said. His view was that the feature that contributes the most to living well is a person's character. Some people just seem to be able to sail through life and overcome any obstacles that they are presented with, while others cannot even handle good fortune. It is a person's character that explains these differences and so if we knew what is involved in developing the best character, we would be using our big brains to provide ourselves with the most useful information.

What is Character?

In watching a movie or reading a novel, we are presented with different individuals, and we see how they act in various situations. As a result we get a reading on the character of the fictional individuals The same thing occurs in non-fictional life. We see our friends and relatives act, and we develop ideas about the kind of people they are. Joe is even-tempered, while Jane is frenetic, and Gertrude is practically comatose. The better we know other people, the more we realize that it is not that easy to characterize them by just a few simple words. Nevertheless, almost everyone has characteristic ways of behaving that provide us with certain expectations of what they will do, and few people are so unpredictable that we are constantly surprised by them.

A person's character consists of combinations of tendencies and inclinations that they have--of character traits. These traits are dispositions, and it will be useful to examine what dispositions are. A disposition is the tendency of an object to behave in a certain way in certain circumstances. Some physical objects have the disposition of reflecting light. That does not mean that they will always be shiny, but it does mean that if they are in a particular set of circumstances, those involved with having light shining on them, the light will bounce back.

Character traits are dispositions in the same sense. If Joe is even-tempered, he has the tendency to act in certain ways in certain situations. When those situations do not occur, then Joe's even-tempered disposition will not be evident. For example, when Joe is sleeping, there is no evidence that he is even-tempered. Even when he is conscious, this trait may not be on display. But there will be those times, when the disposition appears. Say that Joe is driving in heavy traffic, and an excitable driver barely misses him. Some people would start swearing and gesticulating, but not even-tempered Joe. He just smiles to himself, muses on the folly of humanity, and drives on.

Character traits are dispositions, but when it comes to human beings, they do not occur in an automatic way. Even-tempered Joe will not always smile and muse when he is cut off by a frantic driver. There are other actions that even-tempered people may perform in these kinds of situations. They may even not do anything. Also, Joe might even swear and gesture with the right provocation, but that is not his customary way. Character traits then have a statistical aspect to them, as they are the ways people usually act in situations. But there has to be a definite pattern in order to say that a person has a particular trait. o If Joe screamed and threatened at every irritation, it would not make much sense to say that even so, he is really even-tempered. It would be difficult to say he was even-tempered even if Joe went berserk only 20% of the time in the relevant situations. An even-tempered person has to act in a mild way most of the time, although there is no precise point where the attribution of being even-tempered will be withdrawn.

Perfection

What are the best traits to have? The answer is superficially simple: the best traits are those that a person with perfect character would have. But what would a person with perfect character be like? How can we tell when something is perfect?

To get a grasp on this question, consider an example where the concept of perfection is easy to see--a perfect circle. When one tries to draw a free-hand circle, the result is never perfect. In some places wthe figure is too flat, and in others where it bulges too much. The figure could be improved by adding roundness to the flat places, and making the bulges flatter. By a process of adjustment of this type, eventually there will be a perfect figure such that any addition or any subtraction will make the figure less of a circle than it was.

Another example. What would be a perfect cake? Cakes are combinations of ingredients, and we could try various combinations. Some combinations might make the result too sweet or too heavy or too light. By a similar process of adjustment, we might eventually hit on a combination such that when we add a bit more sugar, or subtract a bit more milk, the resulting cake is not as good. This is the sign that we have finally made the perfect cake.

What emerges from these examples is that perfection in anything is a point between excess and deficiency. Perfection is when addition or subtraction makes something worse. This applies to circles, cakes, movies, and anything else. It also applies to traits of character.

Virtues and Vices

With this analysis of perfection Aristotle can discuss the perfect traits of character. The ones that are perfect are called the virtues, and those traits that have either too much or too little are called vices.

'Virtue' is the traditional translation of Aristotle's term 'arete', but 'virtue' may not be the best way to express Aristotle's idea. 'Arete' means excellence without the moral connotation of the word 'virtue'. The best person will have a combination of excellent traits of character, but we would not classify some of them as moral, although that does not indicate that these traits are immoral ones. We consider kindness, honesty and charity to be moral traits and while Aristotle certainly included them on his list of excellent qualities, he included a number of others that we would not classify as moral ones. Examples of this latter group are temperance, sociability and ambition.

The same kind of point applies to what are translated as 'vices.' 'Vice' has the same moral connotation as 'virtue,' and again Aristotle classifies as vices traits we would not consider to be immoral. We do not think that being unambitious or ascetic are immoral. Aristotle's point is that people with these traits do not have the best character, and so do not have good prospects for achieving *eudaimonea*.

An Example--The Virtue of Courage and the Vices of Rashness and Cowardice

Aristotle presented a long and what he considered to be a complete list of traits that the person of perfect character would have. To understand his view, the virtue of courage will be used as an example. Consider the feeling of fear. While fear is a universal aspect of human life, some handle it in an excellent way, and some do not. Those who have the virtue of dealing with fear have the trait of courage, and the associated vices are cowardice and rashness.

Courage is a disposition, which means that it is a way of acting in situations where danger is involved. Usually the danger is physical, but courage can be displayed in other situations. Many people are courageous in situations where there is no danger of physical harm, but there are risks to their social standing, or even to their self-image.

In any case, let us consider the case of someone confronting a physical. Will the courageous person stand firm and face down the danger? Not necessarily, for there are all sorts of factors to consider, such as the degree of danger. There is a huge difference between facing a yapping chihuahua, and being attacked by a rabid German shepherd. Another factor in determining courage is one's own resources. When one is faced with a physical threat, it makes a difference if one is a three hundred pound professional wrestler or a ninety pound pencil-necked geek.

In any situation, the courageous person is able to assess the danger, and their own resources and then take the proper action. A rash person would tend to challenge threats that they cannot really handle; a cowardly person would be too quick to think they had better run away. The matter is complicated because what is courageous for one person in a situation will be rash or cowardly for another in the same situation. What would be courageous for an individual in one case, would be rash in a slightly different case. In each particular situation there is a perfect thing to do given all of the factors, and doing a little less or a little more would make the action less perfect. The courageous person will hit that perfect mark or come close to it more often than will the rash or the cowardly, but it will take very sophisticated judgment and perception to tell what the perfectly courageous thing is to do in any specific case.

Another factor involved in being courageous is the motive that one has for acting. A person might do the perfectly courageous thing, but not to be courageous, but rather to impress one's peers. Or maybe to avoid being shamed. These are not the kinds of actions that Aristotle would say are expressive of courage, even if they are exactly the proper behavior. The motive counts too. So to be courageous, one has to do the right thing, but also with the right motive. It will not be easy.

The Golden Mean

Aristotle provided a list of virtues for various emotions and also for other aspects of life, like telling the truth and giving to charity. He characterized his account as pursuing and finding the Golden Mean, and this phrase has led to some misinterpretations. The term 'mean' usually indicates something like average or moderate—something not too hot and not too cold. Aristotle seems to be saying that we should be average or moderate in our actions and responses—not too loud and not too soft, not too harsh and not too mild. Should we give money to charity? Not too much and not too little. Should we stand up for our rights? Not too forthrightly, but not too hesitantly either. The picture is of someone who is rather mediocre, who does nothing very well, but who floats through life without experiencing any of its high's or low's.

People who attribute this kind of view to Aristotle then proceed to criticize him for having a rather bloodless view, one that no one would really want to accept after thinking about it. However, this account of the Golden Mean does not capture the basic point of Aristotle's approach. For Aristotle the term 'Golden Mean,' did not mean moderation and mediocrity; rather, the Golden Mean is the perfect thing for a particular person to do in a particular situation. The perfect thing may not be the moderate or average thing to do. In some circumstances it may actually be to may actually be to devote one's entire resources to some project—maybe to give up all of one's money, or even to give up one's life. The courageous person is not always the one who fights only moderately, or who leaves when the going gets tough. Sometimes, the courageous person will fight to the death. But not always. The virtue of courage involves knowing when going to the extreme is the perfect thing to do, and then being able to do it.

This shows that the Golden Mean is not always in the center of some particular dimension; sometimes it will be nearer one extreme end of a spectrum, and at other times for other people, it could be at the other end. The Golden Mean is a shifting point, and the person with virtues can hit that moving target. No one is perfect enough to hit it every time, but those who are excellent get close, more often than those who are average, mediocre or corrupt.

Acquiring Virtues-Skills

How do we acquire these excellent traits. How do we get to be courageous, temperate or tactful? The key is that the virtues are skills, and they are acquired in the way that we acquire skills. Consider a skill like playing tennis. How does one improve this ability? Certainly it will help to hit the ball harder, but the best tennis players do not always hit every shot like a cannon. Sometimes the best shot is a soft one just over the net. Also, the best tennis players do not always play all-out on every point. Sometimes they conserve their energy.

Aristotle has some useful suggestions on self-improvement. One important factor for getting better at any skill, be it tennis or virtue, is practice. By repeating an action we generally get better at it. For practice to be really valuable, it helps not to just mindlessly go over an action, but also to be attentive and reflective. If we notice that we are hitting the ball often over the end-line, then we should try to adjust to hit the ball in the court. Analogously, if w see that in dangerous situations, we tend to impulsively jump in, that indicates that we might be better off leaning toward the other end of the spectrum. Attentive practice is valuable, but still the goal is to develop our skill to the point where thinking about it is not necessary. Hopefully, we will become skillful enough so that we just know what would be the right action in the situation, and we then smoothly and almost unconsciously, execute it. That is when our skill is at the highest level--in tennis and in virtue.

There is a special point about practicing at virtue, though, that does not arise with tennis. The actions that we perform in life often lead to pleasure, and that can be problematic in developing excellent traits. Aristotle was by no means an ascetic, and he would have found a monk's life to be almost inhuman, but he did think we have to be very careful about pleasure, because it can be corrupting. Often we perform actions because they feel good, and this can lead to the development of a disposition that is not excellent. We should be careful that we are not just performing actions for the pleasure they bring us.

Another suggestion for improving skills involves observing those who are excellent practitioners. We can often learn a great deal by carefully looking at those who have already achieved a high level of proficiency in some area. Again this is a very complicated process, because observing role-models is not a matter of mindless imitation. For example, the best tennis player in the world may be a tall and powerful man, and you might be a short, slim woman. To try to play tennis exactly the way this man does will not be helpful. Nevertheless, by observing him, there is something to be learned, something useful that can be applied to your own way of playing tennis.

Analogously again, the same holds true in developing virtue. We can read about some eminent person and see how they acted with courage in a difficult situation. There may be very little chance that we would ever be in a similar situation, but still by seeing what they did can be helpful in developing our own courage. How we learn to apply others' actions to our own is a very puzzling fact about human beings, but we all have a great deal of experience that this really does work.

Implications of Aristotle's view

Aristotle's views about virtue have a number of interesting implications. The first is that our character is something that is under our own control. He would have been skeptical of the claim that our personalities and values are stamped in us by the time that we are three years old and there is nothing we can subsequently do about them. But Aristotle was also too good an observer and too sensible to think that our capacity to shape our own character is unlimited. He admitted that if someone were really badly raised, then it might be impossible for them to become virtuous. But those who have had a reasonable up-bringing we can improve their character traits. Trying to do so creates a "virtuous" cycle, for the more we do excellent actions, the more we establish virtuous dispositions, and these make it more likely that we will perform excellent actions.

Aristotle also had an intriguing view about the roles of desires and feelings in human life. For Aristotle the person who has acquired the virtue of courage will not only act appropriately, but the person's feelings will be in line with their actions. This means that a courageous person will tend to feel fear only when it is appropriate to have the feeling. Not only are our actions under our own control, but our feelings are also to some extent. If we begin with the trait of cowardice, we have the feeling of fear much too often, but as we train ourselves to become courageous, we will discover that the feeling of fear itself is not occurring as frequently as it used to. Feelings do not just happen to us according to Aristotle: rather they are like actions in that they result from dispositions, but also they lead to dispositions. There is a "virtuous" cycle with feelings too. Aristotle's advice would be that if we are bothered by feelings that we consider harmful and negative, we need not just suffer or run to the nearest psychopharmacologist. Instead, we can work on our own characters, and by performing the proper actions, the proper feelings will soon develop.

Another interesting implication of concerns the way that Aristotle thinks that we learn skills. He thinks the best way to develop a skill is not by following rigid sets of steps; rather, the process is a more fluid and complex matter of practice and observation. In modern terminology, Aristotle would think that it would be foolish to try to make an algorithm, a recipe, for what to do in order to become virtuous. Precise steps and rules may have some uses in some fields, but they will not be helpful in ethics for there are just too many complicating factors. This doesn't mean it would be impossible to ever make an algorithm for being courageous, but such a set of instructions would be so huge and complex, that they would be of little practical value. The goal in becoming virtuous is similar to the goal of any skill. It is to be able to act smoothly and quickly, to be able to judge instantly what is the best thing to do and then to carry it out. This means having highly developed capacities of perception and judgment, and we do not develop these capacities by learning a set of rules.

One final implication of Aristotle's view concerns his idea of happiness. The whole point of his theory is to achieve happiness, eudaimonea. This is the reason ultimately to develop the virtues, as he thought that they would contribute greatly to our capacity to achieve eudaimonea. So while it is always a good thing to develop a prized skill to a high degree, the point of doing so is not just the achievement itself. In Aristotle's view, based on his observations, the more virtues that we have, the happier we will probably be.

But there is a tricky aspect to this. If we are virtuous, we will be happier, but if we consciously try to adopt the virtues in order to be happier, then we will not gain them. A courageous person will be

82

happier than a coward or a reckless goof, but in being courageous, the person has to act from the motive of being courageous and not from the motive of being happier. If one does achieve courage, then happiness will trail along as a by-product, but happiness is not the kind of thing that one can achieve directly. Apparently, we only achieve it if we do not think about it very much.

This point seems to follow from the nature of attention. If a tennis player wants to get better so that she can win championships, and thinks mainly of that, then the attention that she needs to devote to improving her skill will be missing. She will not be focussing on improving her backhand, but instead she will be thinking of the great feeling she will have holding up the championship trophy and being applauded by the crowd. Thus, she will probably not focus enough on improving her backhand, and she will never win the trophy. On the other hand, if she concentrates on improving her backhand, the championships are more likely to come in due course.

This has a clear application to the relation of the virtues and happiness. If we just think of the happiness that will come when we have finally achieved courage, temperance and tactfulness, then we will probably never develop them to a high degree. But if we really forget everything else and concentrate on achieving these virtues, then we probably will be happy. This aspect of Aristotle's view has a Zen-like quality to it, for he was saying that the way to be happy, which is after our main goal, is to not think about being happy.

Answers to the two original questions

At the beginning it was said that Aristotle was trying to answer two questions: 'What is the best way to live?' and 'How can one determine what is the right thing to do when it is not obvious?'

We have focused so far almost entirely on answering the first question. In general the answer is that the best life is one that will result in happiness and that will involve matters of chance, but also some matters that are under our own control. We should endeavor to have a life that engages our capacities for reason. In particular it will help to use reason to see what is involved in developing excellent traits of character, because they contribute more to happiness than any other factor that we can control.

But what about the second question? Nothing explicit has been said about how Aristotle would answer that one, and the reason is that the answer is already contained in the first answer. If we develop the virtues, then we will be able to determine what is the right thing to do in difficult situations. Other philosophers have thought that there must be some system of rules, some algorithm, some set of steps, for generating the solutions to difficult moral problems. But Aristotle disagreed, for he said that ethics is not like geometry. He thought that it would be futile to try to develop a system that will cover all of the kinds of situation that will arise and provide an answer for all of them. Aristotle would have thought that trying to find a decision procedure for Ethics will never really work.

But what should be done when we face moral dilemmas, when we have to make a choice, and none of the available alternatives seems to be very satisfactory? Should we help others, sacrificing our own projects, or tell the others to help themselves? How far should we go in protesting unjust activities by our own democratically elected government? Should fetal tissue be used to save the lives of adults? These and other problems bedevil serious thinkers even after developing elaborate ethical systems. Aristotle's view is that no system of rules will provide a satisfactory conclusion to these dilemmas. The best that we can do is to work on our virtues, develop our characters, and then we will be able to judge and perceive what should be done. This is the best that can be done.

Plato's Objection-To Be Good it is Necessary to Articulate What is Good

Aristotle presented his views in a straight-forward manner, and he never explicitly raised objections to his view. To understand Aristotle's ideas more clearly, it is useful to think of how someone like Plato might object to them.

While Aristotle did criticize Plato's ideas concerning what is good, there is no record of Plato's response, if he had any. Still, given what Plato said in his many writings, a Platonic objection to Aristotle can certainly be imagined, and it is clear Plato would have been critical because Aristotle never explicitly defined or articulated what is good. In Plato's view, before one can do what is right, or live a good life, one has to provide an explicit account of what the good and the right are. Otherwise, one does not know that one is living well or acting in the right way. This is the point of many of Plato's dialogues in which Socrates, who represents Plato's view, shows that people cannot be pious, just or good if they cannot define these notions. To know what is good mean being able to define 'goodness' and defend the definition against objections. Plato thought that being able to convincingly articulate an account of what is good in the abstract is necessary for doing what is good. He also thought that this kind of knowledge was sufficient for being good, because if one knew what was good, one would automatically do it.

To illustrate Plato's point, consider a good parent. In Plato's view we could not really be a good parent unless we had found the definition of goodness, and having found that out, we would be able to apply the concept to how to raise our children in the proper way. But without an explicit grasp of the concept of goodness, we will not really know how to be good parents. Of course, this kind of explicit account of goodness in itself will be very theoretical and will be extremely difficult to obtain. But if we are serious about being good parents, then we must be willing to exert ourselves to get this critically important, knowledge, for once we have the knowledge, we will necessarily apply it.

Aristotle's answer to these criticisms would be based on the distinction that he made between theory and practice. Living well and doing the right actions are practical matters, and theoretical knowledge is neither necessary nor sufficient for successful actions. Being a great physicist and knowing how sound waves are produced will not automatically make one a great violin player. Neither will mastering the best books about violin technique. There is no substitute in practical matters for actual practice.

Theoretical knowledge is not sufficient for excellent practice, but Aristotle would also argue that it is not necessary. Explaining what one is doing is quite a different skill than being an excellent practitioner. Many people who are excellent at what they do, be it raising children, hitting a tennis ball or playing the violin also happen to be somewhat inarticulate. This does not mean that they are unintelligent or unreflective; it just means that they are not skilled at expressing in language what makes them so excellent. When Willie Mays, the great baseball player, was asked how he was able to turn his back when the ball was hit and run to the spot where the ball would land. he responded. "I don't analyze 'em; I just catch 'em."

Plato's viws led to a search for what he called the Form of the Good--the basic common essence of all good things. He claimed in *The Republic*, that one could only find out what the Form of the Good is after decades of the most rigorous study . Aristotle also believed that becoming a virtuous person would also take time. for in order to develop the best dispositions, a great deal of practice is necessary. But to pursuing the Form of the Good would not be that helpful. It would be much better to be actually living a human life, inter-acting with others, facing dangers and expressing pleasure. for that is the way that people actually become virtuous.

But this point should not be pushed too far, for Aristotle he did not think that an intellectual understanding was completely irrelevant. Certainly, it can help to have some theoretical understanding of an activity to become better at it. But this theoretical understanding is not necessary.

Finally, Plato thought that knowledge of what is good is critical. because once one knows what is good, one will necessarily do it. His view was that everyone acts according to what they think is the best thing to do, but since people do not know what is best, they often act in ways that are wrong or harmful. to themselves and others. It is not that people are wicked; they are just ignorant. So a self-indulgent person really thinks that his actions are for the best, or at least the person thinks so when he is performing them. Later, the person might realize he made a mistake. but at the moment of action, the person had the belief, mistaken as it was, that drinking this whole bottle of vodka was the best alternative available to him at the time. But if the person knew that some other action was better—really knew that—then the bottle of vodka would have remained on the shelf. This is why Plato thought that knowing the good is sufficient for performing the good.

Aristotle discusses this same issue in the *Nichomachean Ethics*. and he has a much more common sense view. and one that seems to fit our observations of people much more closely than does Plato's view. Aristotle said that some people act badly, not because they are ignorant, but because they are weak. This is the condition that he called *akrasia*. which is usually translated as weakness of the will. Plato did not think that there was any such condition, but Aristotle thought that it was quite common and very apparent. Still, it is a puzzling phenomenon that requires analysis and explanation, and Aristotle devoted a good deal of attention to it in the *Nichomachean Ethics*. Weakness of the will is a gross failure of rationality for people know that something is bad for them, all things considered, and still they do it. An adequate psychology would have to show how weakness of the will is possible, and Aristotle tried to provide that. Whether his account was successful is still being discussed, but in any case, it would seem that any psychology that says there is no such condition, as Plato's did, would be much more difficult to accept as an adequate view.

Rest of the Ethics

The *Nichomachean Ethics* is quite a large book, and what has been provided so far, is just an account of some of the main issues. Aristotle wanted to provide a complete account of the virtues, and so he presented a complete list of them, with a discussion of each one.

There are also a number of other topics that Aristotle examined that are related in various ways to the main issues. He provided a careful analysis of voluntary actions, because it is voluntary actions that are crucial in the development of our dispositions. He also included a discussion of the different kinds of justice, as acting justly was a very significant matter in Greek morality (as it is for us too), as well as a careful analysis of the different kinds of friendship. Because happiness and pleasure are such important concepts in Aristotle's view of ethics, he also had an extensive section devoted to examining them. One other topic that was discussed was what would be the absolutely happiest life for a human being. Like his teacher Plato, Aristotle had arguments that purported to prove that the life of a philosopher, devoted to contemplation, would ultimately produce the greatest eudaimonea for a human being. So while Aristotle thought that one could have a flourishing life without theoretical knowledge, nevertheless, his view was that studying abstract theory, and in particular contemplating the unmoved mover is the greatest happiness a person can possibly have.

9
Politics

The Greek city-states were quite small by modern standards, and had many features that would strike us as strange, and probably repugnant. Slavery was taken for granted in all of them, and the roles of men and women were very distinct: men ran the cities, and women stayed home. In fact, women were not even considered to be citizens.

Aristotle, unlike his teacher Plato, never raised any serious criticisms of these features of Greek social organization. To the contrary, he defended them as natural and necessary. This may lead us to think that Aristotle's political views should be immediately disqualified for serious consideration, but that would be a hasty and ungenerous conclusion. In spite of all the differences and changes that have occurred over the centuries, there are many interesting and insightful things that Aristotle had to say about politics.

Relation of the Politics to the Ethics

At the very beginning of Aristotle's *Ethics*, he mentioned that a complete account of the best way for a person to live would require a discussion of politics. In Aristotle's work, *Politics*, he explained why this is so, and the reason is that he believed that human beings could only live a good life if they were part of an organized political community. Aristotle thought that the Greek city-state organization was the best kind for human beings, but what is of more interest to us is his general view concerning why people have to be part of a political organization in order to have *eudaimonea*.

The first point of this argument is that people are social by nature. Human beings cannot live well by themselves. For Aristotle, the kind of creature that can flourish living completely on its own has to be either a beast or a god, for such a creature clearly cannot be a human being. We are not self-sufficient creatures as we have needs that we need others to satisfy--reproductive needs, emotional needs, and even material ones

The best evidence for our inherent social nature is the existence of human language. For Aristotle language is fundamentally an instrument of communication--we use it to tell others what we are thinking about and to hear their thoughts, to change others and to be changed by them. The one-year old baby begins to speak in the same way that he begins to walk--more or less on his own, as an expression of impulses that are part of a human life. We are creatures who walk upright, and we are also creatures that speak to each other. Both aspects are part of our nature, but language can only develop in a community of language-users.

Political Communities

From the *Ethics* we know that our big brains are the special feature of human beings, and that they provide us with our outstanding ability to reason. We have also just seen that we have social needs that are part of our inherent nature. Aristotle used these two points to show that we will flourish best when we are in a community where we can use this reasoning capacity to help organize the community itself so that it will satisfy our needs and enable us to develop our capacities to the utmost. Aristotle thought that the city-state was a political organization that had just the right size and constitution for this purpose. Other kindss of human association are either too big or too small. For example, Aristotle does say that the family is the most basic form of human community, but it is not big enough to be the kind of group that will satisfy all of one's needs. Just from a material point of view, it is very limited, but also its small size would stifle many interests a person would have. One's partner and children might be curious, witty and stimulating, but it is unlikely that they will be interested in everything that we want to talk about and do.

The association of families in a village will be more helpful for fulfilling some of our human needs and this is the next stage in Aristotle's account of the development of human association, but small villages and towns, for all of their charm, can also be stifling and limiting. The place where people can really develop and flourish is an association of villages, which is what Aristotle considered the typical Greek city-state to be. A city-state had just the right size. It was big enough to provide all the stimulation and contact with others that a person could desire, and yet it was not so big that one would become lost and unable to have any impact on the way the community was organized and run. Aristotle was aware that there was a higher level of organization than the city-state, the nation, and the Persian Empire was his model for this kind of human association. But he thought that living in a nation would frustrating, because there would be little opportunity to use one's big brain to have an effect on the nation's laws and institutions.

This last point is of great importance to Aristotle's view of politics. He thought that the best life is one where people are actively involved in the devising the basic features of their own community. This does not mean that he was for participatory democracy and that he thought that every person in the city should have some voice in the important decisions. He definitely did not have that view. But he did think that all things being equal, the life of a person who is involved in the important decisions of their own group will have a more fulfilled life than the person who removes themselves from these decisions and just lets their life be run by others. One of our human capacities is the ability to arrange our society. Someone who develops and uses this capacity will live a better life than someone who does not.

On this point Aristotle had a very different view than the one expressed by his teacher, Plato, *The Republic*. Plato thought that the best life would be one of pure philosophical contemplation. Participating in the political life of one's city is something that may be necessary for the good of others, but it would be something a person would wish to avoid if they really understood things. Plato, unlike Aristotle, did not see participating in politics as a feature of life that expressed our inner needs and that was fulfilling in itself.

Features of Political Communities

A good deal of Aristotle's book, *Politics*, is devoted to a very exhaustive and exhausting study of the variety of forms of political communities. Aristotle seems to have been familiar with the details of every city-state in Greece, and he realized that while they might fit into some broad categories, each one has unique characteristics due to factors of history, geography and population size. Still, there were some common patterns that could be discerned. The most significant feature in classifying types of political communities was the number of people involved in the actual rule of the city. The alternatives in this regard were one ruler, a few, or many, and these three possibilities corresponded to three kinds of governments--kingship, aristocracy and what he called polity. These are the names that Aristotle provided for the three kinds of governments when they were well-run, but each one was subject to its own kind of corruption. As a matter of fact, the actual forms of government that existed in Greece at his time were most often the corrupt forms that were called tyranny, oligarchy and democracy. Aristotle provided many details about how each of these forms can decay, and also what makes them flourish. In this discussion, it is apparent he believed that we should pay special attention to certain general features of political association.

Hierarchy

For Aristotle any association between people to fulfill some common purpose requires a hierarchy, except interestingly, for friendship. This is the case in the small groups like the family and in bigger communities like the city-state. Someone has to be the one to decide and someone else has to be the one to carry out the decision. He does acknowledge that the ruling role does not always have to be carried out by the same individuals, and that the different roles can be exchanged, as occurs in the democratic forms. But nevertheless, there have to be leaders and followers in every human organization.

He supported this view by claiming that people have different natural endowments. Some individuals are just natural leaders and some are born to the followers. But even if we discount Aristotle's view about the natural origin of this difference, he might still have a point that hierarchy is an unavoidable feature of human groups. We can certainly see this characteristic in the behavior of social animals, but it could be objected that there is no other possibility for them, because they do not have the capacities of language that would be necessary for developing an egalitarian structure. But observation shows that human groups also have a hierarchical form. One sees it in businesses, unions, governments, universities, clubs, families (at least with parents and children), religions, and even in theologies (God and the subservient angels.) Maybe one explanation for this ever-present hierarchy is the efficiency of a division of labor.

Justice, Stability and Education

But there is another opposing feature of human groups that is just as significant, and that is the interest in justice. One of results of our ability to speak with each other is that we can discuss what is just. We all have the same basic idea of justice, which is that people should be treated equally, but equal in what respect? Clearly we are not equal in strength, talent, virtue or wealth. So what is it that counts? This is a critical matter, for it is disputes on this particular issue that are the cause of most of the difficulties that can be found in political associations.

Aristotle thought that people were treated justly when each person is given the share that they deserve. But of course, that just leads to the problem of how to determine what a person deserves. The rich will think that wealth is the most important criterion of desert, and the poor will disagree. The intelligent and educated will argue for their specific merit, but those without them will say that they are irrelevant. In a political community there will have to be some form of hierarchy, but there will also be a discussion and probably a dispute, about what form of hierarchy is just.

But if the dispute on this basic issue becomes too ferocious, then there is likely to be a great deal of instability in the political organization, and in that case, the very reason for forming such an organization will be lost. When a community is up in arms over whether their hierarchy is just or not, the community will undoubtedly not be fulfilling its function of providing for the needs of the people in it, and in particular. the features necessary for a good life will be missing.

The point that Aristotle was making is that there has to be a certain amount of agreement about the basic values. if the community is to remain stable enough to fulfill its function. That does not mean that everyone has to agree about everything. or that people should be very much alike. A certain amount of diversity is also necessary if the city-state is to fulfill its various functions. But if there is disagreement on some fundamental issue. then there is trouble. If a good portion of the community thinks that slavery is a necessary element for the health of the group. and another portion thinks that it is unjustifiably immoral. then there will be dissension and even civil war.

Stability is essential for the community fulfilling its function. but it does not follow that Aristotle would have approved of every stable city-state. Stability does require agreement on values, but he would disagree with saying that it did not matter what values were agreed upon. The political community is supposed to provide for the development of human excellence. and it would be unlikely that a community that unanimously agrees about Nazi values would contribute to its members achieving eudaimonea as described in the *Ethics*.

How do we get the members of our community to have the same basic values that will lead to stability? Aristotle thought that this is the purpose of education. and he would not entrust it to the parents of the community's children. This matter is too important. parents are too diverse in their own values and too uninformed to accomplish this task. It is the political leaders who should make sure that the children are inculcated with the proper values. In the *Politics* Aristotle presents a curriculum that will yield the sought-after results.

Is this just a form of brain-washing? Not necessarily, for Aristotle thought that when the children are older. explanations and justifications for the values taught could be given. But he thought that these explanations will only really be effective if people have developed the right dispositions, and waiting until adulthood to do that is probably too late. For Aristotle it is not just philosophical argument that lead to the actions and values that are needed to support the community. Childhood training is more important.

10
Aesthetics

While all that we know about Aristotle, and his fellow philosophers, comes to us in the form of writing, it is ironic that writing itself played a very small role in Greek culture. One reason for this is that before the printing press, writing was expensive and laborious. Words, spoken by a human being in one's presence, were the main medium of political discussion and persuasion, as well being the basis of literature. For the Greeks, many of whom who were undoubtedly illiterate, their contact with the works of Homer was hearing them declaimed by bards in the market-place. Drama, comedy and tragedy, were directly experienced in their theatres, and were not studied as texts.

Aristotle, with his encyclopedic interests, saw this area of life of deserving his attention and he devoted a substantial portion of his powers to the examination and understanding of the uses of speech in these contexts. In his works, *The Rhetoric* and *The Poetics*, Aristotle undertook to identify the best examples of speeches and drama's and also to explain how they achieved their effects.

Rhetoric

The Greeks spent a great deal of time listening and composing speeches. They heard them during trials, in the discussions of what to do that went on in the political assembly, and on numerous ceremonial occasions. These kinds of situations provided Aristotle with his major classification of speeches--political, forensic (the legal kind) and ceremonial.

He had a great deal to say about each kind, and especially about the political and the forensic, but in general he thought that speeches were composed of two basic elements. They are what can be called the logical aspect, in which the speaker presents his case and his arguments to support his conclusion, and emotional aspect, by which the speaker persuades the audience to accept the conclusion that he is arguing for. As one reads *The Rhetoric* it is not completely clear if Aristotle thought that the emotional element was an unfortunate necessary evil that speakers would have to include to be successful. At points Aristotle said that what is really important is the logic of the case, the soundness of the reasoning and the truth of the premises, but at others he indicated that the emotional appeal of a speech is essential too.

Aristotle did spend a great deal of time talking about the logical aspect, but much of what he had to say about logic was already covered in his other works. What is of special interest in *The Rhetoric* is his discussion of the emotions. He said that to be effective, a good speaker would have to understand the structure of human emotions, how to arouse them and also how to dissipate them, and to help speakers in this regard, Aristotle provided an analysis of some of the most important human emotions.

Emotions

The discussion of the emotions occurs in Book II of *The Rhetoric* and it is an acute and brilliant analysis of a topic that philosophers, being so concerned with reason, typically just mention with a few dismissive remarks. Plato did discuss the emotions, sometimes in great detail, but he often gave the impression that he thought emotions were an unfortunate aspect of human existence, and are usually blind and urgent impulses, originating in the corrupt physical body, that have to be strictly controlled by reason. Most subsequent philosophers accepted Plato's general view and then provided their own particular variation of it.

However, Aristotle was quite distinctive, in that he thought that emotions were anything but simple impulses, and his analysis is anything but dismissive of them. As Aristotle presented them, the emotions are very complex states, involving feelings of pleasure and

pain, but also involving judgments and beliefs. and contextual factors
of a very subtle kind.

Fear and Pity

To provide a taste of Aristotle's analysis. we will consider some of
the things he said about pity and fear, two emotions that were of
importance in his discussion of tragedy. The usual view is that pity and
fear are feelings of a distinctive type. and that we distinguish these
emotions by how they feel to us. But Aristotle thought otherwise. His
account of fear does say that it is a pain or a disturbance, but that is
only part of state of fear, and given what he focused on in his
discussion of fear. the painful feeling part of it is not the most
significant factor. What is of more importance is that the painful
feeling is due to a mental picture of some destructive or painful evil in
the future. But Aristotle refined this even further. because we do not
feel fear for those destructive evils that we think are in the distant
future. Fear occurs only when we believe that the destructive evil is
close at hand. And then this can be refined even further. What leads to
fear is not only the judgment that something destructive is nearby. but
also the belief that there is not much we can do to prevent it. Other
matters can also effect whether fear occurs. People who have already
experienced a great number of horrors often become callous. and so the
prospect of another terrible thing does not frighten them as much.

The result is that fear turns out to be a state that includes a number
of judgments about what the situation is. what one's own resources are.
and that is affected to a great degree by one's experiences and
character. Whether a person will experience fear is no simple matter,
for all of these factors play a part in this complex state. Further, if any
of the factors are missing, the fear should disappear too. For example.
a person might be afraid an approaching storm. but if the person finds
out that they are not helpless and that there are things to be done to
possibly limit the coming destruction, the fear should decrease. and
maybe even be extinguished. Another condition that can affect the
existence of fear or its intensity for a person is the kind of training that
they have had. Given the right sort of experiences. fear might no
longer affect them as it used to. They may have developed beliefs that
the destructive evils are actually very far away, or that they really are
not so evil. or as happens with unfortunate people, so many other bad

things have happened, that nothing more can be considered to be that destructive.

One other interesting point about Aristotle's discussion of fear is that he said that it has a close relationship to pity. Generally, he said, what causes us to feel fear is what causes us to feel pity when it happens to another. What this indicates is that Aristotle did not think that pity and fear are to be distinguished by the particular kind of internal feeling they produce, but rather by the other factors--who is facing the danger, how close is it, how helpless is the person, etc.

Aristotle's discussion of emotions should be of great value to speakers who are interested in affecting the emotions of their audiences. When a speaker understands what provokes fear, and also what dissipates it, and what its significant features of actually are, then the speaker is in a position to compose his speech to achieve the effect he desires. Aristotle's shrewd, subtle and insightful account of the emotions is very helpful in this regard.

Poetics

The Poetics is a short work in which Aristotle presented his definitions of various literary genres and then discussed the characteristics the best examples of these genres would have. In particular, he discussed tragic drama and epic poetry and even provided rules for poets to follow in composing them. These rules may seem rather arbitrary to us, such as the best tragedy would confine its action to one location, and some of his rules, such as his discussion of what meters should be used, are no longer be of great interest to most contemporary readers of *The Poetics*.

Nevertheless, Aristotle raised a major question that is still very puzzling and that is difficult to answer. The question is, why do we find tragic dramas to be so enthralling. For Aristotle, a tragic drama meant the performance of play, in which the actors wore masks, and there were elements of rhythm, dance, poetry and music. Tragedy has taken somewhat different forms for us--movies, television productions, novels, as well as what we see in theatres. But still the question remains, why do we have such great interest in these tragic forms. What function do they perform for us? Aristotle raised this issue in *The Poetics*, and provided two sorts of answers to it, one general and one specific.

Aristotle's general answer is that tragedies, as are all dramatic presentations, are imitations of actual occurrences, and because of our nature, they appeal to us for that reason. Imitation, Aristotle says, is natural to human beings and it has two different aspects. First, we are the most imitative creatures in the world and that is the way we all begin to learn, for example, that is the way a baby begins speaking its native language. The second reason is more relevant to the question about tragedy, and that is that we take delight in works of imitation. We simply enjoy seeing representations of real things, even if the real things are horrible, such as low animals, bugs, or dead bodies.

Aristotle said that this second point can be shown by experience, and it is not difficult to think of many examples to support his claim. But he was not satisfied to just point out the fact that we delight in imitations, but he also presented an explanation for it. According to Aristotle, the delight stems from the fact that when we see an imitation of something, we are learning, and learning is the greatest of pleasures, not just for philosophers, but for the rest of humanity too. He did not say in what way an imitation promotes learning except to briefly and cryptically remark that it enables us to "gather the meaning of things".

In this specific passage Aristotle was referring to the representative nature of pictures, but what he said is supposed to apply to all forms of art, and especially dramatic performances. Aristotle's point is obscure here, although we can certainly agree with him that we do take a fundamental delight in seeing things and actions being represented. But how exactly is learning involved? Perhaps what he was getting at was that in a picture or a drama, we notice features that are part of reality that we might have ignored, and this provides an addition to our knowledge, and thus provides the joy of learning. So, in seeing a picture of a horse, the artist's emphasis of the strong musculature would cause us to look at actual horses, and focus more on how their powerful muscles are organized to enable them to run so fast.

If this is what Aristotle meant, there is a point to it, and we can see how it could apply to tragic drama. We go to such performances just for the sheer pleasure of seeing an imitation of actual actions, but also the play itself might make us think about the nature of human life by pointing out features we normally overlook. While these features may be depressing in themselves, there is a certain amount of pleasure in the realization that yes, that is the way life is.

Catharsis

The more specific answer that Aristotle gave about our interest in tragedy is that he said that by arousing pity and fear, it provides a catharsis of such emotions. Aristotle just mentioned the cathartic effect, and he did not explain the details of how this effect is achieved and why it would be a reason to attend tragic plays.

Still, it is not difficult to see the general idea that Aristotle had in mind. We all enter the theater with fears, anxieties and worries, and somehow by seeing the representation of a character who undergoes much worse problems than we are facing, and who is defeated by them, we discharge some of our own anxieties and feel cleansed. By attending tragedies, people find relief from the things that are bothering them.

But does Aristotle's theory provide the best answer for why we feel uplifted after seeing tragedies? Why would seeing someone else come to grief remove our own anxieties about whether we will suffer and lose? If anything, it would seem to heighten our fears, for if we see people as talented and as accomplished as Oedipus and Hamlet failing, then what can we expect to happen to someone more ordinary like ourselves?

Perhaps the cathartic effect is supposed to work by seeing someone greater than ourselves laid low, and this comforts us by seeing that even those people have problems they cannot also overcome. This is a possible mechanism for how catharsis might work, but it does not really fit what Aristotle said, because the catharsis is supposed to relieve us of the pain of fear and pity, and this possible explanation does not pertain to the fear and pity we might be experiencing. Fear, Aristotle said in *The Rhetoric* concerned the disturbances and pain we have because of the prospect that some evil will occur to us. Seeing that evils occur to others greater than we are would not seem to be the kind of thing that will lessen our own disturbances.

Besides not providing an account of how and why the catharsis works, it is also not that convincing that a catharsis of fear and pity is the reason we attend tragic dramas. There is undoubtedly something that attracts us about this kind of play, but is it really that we feel purified and relieved of our own fears afterward? Aristotle's specific answer does not seem that plausible, but still the question that he raised is a puzzling and intriguing one.

Bibliography

Aristotle, The Complete Works, (ed. J.Barnes), Princeton, 1984 (two volumes)

Ackrill, J.L., *Aristotle the Philosopher*, Oxford University Press, 1981

Allan, DJ, *The Philosophy of Aristotle*, Oxford, 1970

Barnes, Jonathan, *Aristotle*, Oxford University Press, 1982

Barnes, Jonathan ed., *The Cambridge Companion to Aristotle*, Cambridge, 1995

Barnes, J, Schofield, M., Sorabji, R., *Articles on Aristotle*, Duckworth, 1975 (4 volumes),

Charlton, W., ed., *Physics*, Oxford, 1970

Clagett, Marshall, *Greek Science in Antiquity*, London, 1957

Frede, Michael, *Essays in Ancient Philosophy*, Oxford, 1987

Gill, M.L. Aristotle on Substance: the Paradox of Unity, Princeton, 1989

Graham, D, Aristotle's two Systems, Oxford, 1987

Irwin, Terence, *Aristotle's First Principles*, Clarendon Press, 1988

Jaeger, Werner, *Aristotle: Fundamentals of the History of His Development*, Clarendon Press, 1948

Lear, Jonathan, *Aristotle; the Desire to Understand*, Cambridge University, 1988

Lloyd, G.E.R., *Aristotle: the Growth & Structure of his Thought*, Cambridge, 1968

Matthen, Mohan, *Aristotle Today*, Academic Printing, 1986

Ross, Sir David, *Aristotle*, Methuen, 1923

Veatch, Henry, *Aristotle: A Contemporary Appreciation*, Indiana University Press, 1974

Wiggins, David, *Sameness and Substance*, Oxford, 1980

THE WADSWORTH PHILOSOPHERS SERIES is dedicated to providing both philosophy students and general readers with insight into the background, development, and thinking of great intellects throughout the history of civilization. More than a simple guide, each of the volumes has the goal of helping to empower the reader when analyzing and discussing original works. For North American college and university adopters, any of these volumes may be bundled with each other or with any other Wadsworth titles at a substantial discount. They are also excellent companions to, and may be bundled with, Daniel Kolak's *The Philosophy Source*, a CD-ROM that provides ready access to over 100 classic, primary readings. Contact your local Wadsworth representative for bundling assistance. For more details about this series, *The Philosophy Source* CD-ROM, and other related titles, join us at **www.cengage.com/philosophy**

Volumes in the series include:

Made in the USA
Middletown, DE
16 April 2018